by Joel Lurie Grishaver & Jane Golub

Artwork by Lane Yerkes, Christine Tripp
Mark Robert Halper & David Bleicher

Siddur Mastery & Meaning
Volume 1

We wish to thank
Melanie Berman, Micha'el Akiba,
Debi Rowe and Lifsa Schachter,
who worked with us and offered
invaluable insights on this project.

ISBN #1-891662-10-4

Copyright © 2001 Torah Aura Productions Second Edition 2007
Artwork © Christine Tripp
Artwork © Lane Yerkes
Icon Photographs © Mark Robert Halper

Torah Aura Productions • 4423 Fruitland Avenue, Los Angeles, CA 90058

(800) BE-Torah • (800) 238-6724 (585-7312) • fax (323) 585-0327

E-MAIL <misrad@torahaura.com> • Visit the Torah Aura website at www.torahaura.com

MANUFACTURED IN CHINA

Open My Lips

אֲדֹנָי שְׂפָתַי תִּפְתָּח וּפִי יַגִּיד תְּהִלָּתֶךָ

(Psalms 51.15)

The Work of the Heart

nce, Jews offered sacrifices in the Temple. These sacrifices were called עֲבוֹדָה, work. When prayers replaced sacrifice, they were called עֲבוֹדַת הַלֵּב, the work of the heart. כַּוָּנָה means aiming or pointing. By adding כַּוָּנָה, our prayers become more than just words we say—they bring us closer to God. One needs to learn how to read and understand Hebrew prayers and where to point one's heart while one is praying. That is how we do עֲבוֹדַת הַלֵּב.

This is a story from the Baal Shem Tov, the first <u>H</u>asidic teacher, about כַּוָּנָה, heart pointing.

There was a king who loved music. The king had a court musician who played beautifully. But after a time, the musician got tired of playing the same thing over and over. Every time the king asked for his favorite song it had less and less life in it. The musician told the king, "I am having a hard time being excited about this song. I have played it too many times."

3

The king had an idea. He brought in a guest and asked the musician to play his favorite song especially for this guest. The guest made the difference. The music was again filled with feeling and meaning.

Every day the king brought in a different guest, and the musician played the song with new excitement. But, eventually, the king ran out of new people to be guests. With no one new to hear it, the music became old and tired again.

The king thought and thought and came up with a new idea. He blindfolded the musician and told him a new guest was there to hear his music. The musician imagined the guest, and his playing was again filled with spirit. The king did this every day, and every day the musician found the כַּוָּנָה with which to play the king's favorite song.

Questions
1. Why is it hard to do the same thing over and over?
2. How do you trick yourself into finding something new about things you do over and over?
3. How does this story help you understand where to point your heart when you start to pray?

In this book you will learn to
- recite a number of Hebrew prayers
- understand some of the vocabulary and root words
- know the stories and meaning behind those prayers.

 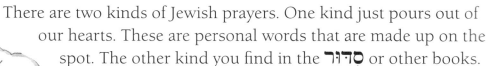

What is a בְּרָכָה?

There are two kinds of Jewish prayers. One kind just pours out of our hearts. These are personal words that are made up on the spot. The other kind you find in the סִדּוּר or other books. At the heart of most of these book prayers is the word בָּרוּךְ.

A בְּרָכָה is a prayer that either begins or ends with a sentence that starts with the word בָּרוּךְ. The word בְּרָכָה actually means three different things:

- A בְּרָכָה is a gift from God. A person can say, "I have been *blessed* with good health," or "I have been *blessed* with a wonderful family."

- A בְּרָכָה is also a "thank you" to God for a gift that we have received. That is why we say prayers like "*Praised* are You Who gives strength to those who are tired."

- A בְּרָכָה is also a request for a gift from God. In every morning service Jews say, "Grant us peace... the One Who *blesses* Israel with peace."

In order to really mean a בְּרָכָה in our hearts we need to

- notice the gifts that we have been given,

- believe that God is the source of those gifts.

A בְּרָכָה is not just words. It is a connection to God.

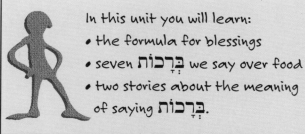

In this unit you will learn:
- the formula for blessings
- seven בְּרָכוֹת we say over food
- two stories about the meaning of saying בְּרָכוֹת.

Some Basic בְּרָכוֹת

Do you know these Hebrew words? They will help you understand the בְּרָכוֹת below.

Your teacher will help you review or learn these Hebrew words. They will help you understand the blessings at the bottom of the page.

You teacher will also explain that יי is pronounced אֲדֹנָי

פֵּירוֹת   פְּרִי הַגֶּפֶן   לֶחֶם

מְזוֹנוֹת   עֵץ   בְּשָׂמִים

Can you figure out over what each בְּרָכָה is said? (Guessing is good.)

1. בָּרוּךְ אַתָּה יי אֱלֹהֵינוּ מֶלֶךְ הָעוֹלָם הַמּוֹצִיא לֶחֶם מִן הָאָרֶץ.

2. בָּרוּךְ אַתָּה יי אֱלֹהֵינוּ מֶלֶךְ הָעוֹלָם בּוֹרֵא פְּרִי הַגָּפֶן.

3. בָּרוּךְ אַתָּה יי אֱלֹהֵינוּ מֶלֶךְ הָעוֹלָם בּוֹרֵא פְּרִי הָעֵץ.

4. בָּרוּךְ אַתָּה יי אֱלֹהֵינוּ מֶלֶךְ הָעוֹלָם בּוֹרֵא מִינֵי בְשָׂמִים.

5. בָּרוּךְ אַתָּה יי אֱלֹהֵינוּ מֶלֶךְ הָעוֹלָם בּוֹרֵא מִינֵי מְזוֹנוֹת.

Every בְּרָכָה begins with these words:

בָּרוּךְ אַתָּה יי אֱלֹהֵינוּ מֶלֶךְ הָעוֹלָם

1. בָּרוּךְ פְּרִי מֶלֶךְ הָעוֹלָם מִינֵי בּוֹרֵא לֶחֶם

2. הַגֶּפֶן אֱלֹהֵינוּ לֶחֶם הָאָרֶץ הָעֵץ אַתָּה פְּרִי

3. בְּשָׂמִים הַמּוֹצִיא הָאָרֶץ מִינֵי אֱלֹהֵינוּ בָּרוּךְ

Recite some phrases with these בְּרָכָה words.

4. בּוֹרֵא פְּרִי הָעֵץ   אֱלֹהֵינוּ מֶלֶךְ הָעוֹלָם   בּוֹרֵא מִינֵי

5. בָּרוּךְ אַתָּה   הַמּוֹצִיא לֶחֶם מִן הָאָרֶץ   בּוֹרֵא מִינֵי בְשָׂמִים

6. בּוֹרֵא פְּרִי הַגֶּפֶן   בָּרוּךְ אַתָּה יי   מִן הָאָרֶץ   מֶלֶךְ הָעוֹלָם

Now that you've practiced, why don't you take a second try at reciting the blessings on page 6.

עֲצֹר!

בְּרָכָה A Word Search

Find the בְּרָכָה words in this word search:

בּוֹרֵא	אֶרֶץ
הַמּוֹצִיא	אַתָּה
מֶלֶךְ	מִינֵי
פְּרִי	עֵץ
אֲדָמָה	לֶחֶם
עוֹלָם	בָּרוּךְ

Word search grid:

הַ	מ		וּ	צִ	י	א	בְּ
אֱ	דְ	מָ	ה	עֵ	ם	ס	ר
פְּ	ה	אֱ	רֵ	צ	ח	וּ	
בְ	וּ	רֵ	א	מֶ	ל	דְ	
ע	וּ	לָ	ם	לֶ	חֶ	פְּ	
בְּ	רֵ	אַ	תָּ	ה	ם	רְ	
לְ	א	תָּ	מִ	י	נֵ	י	

7

Benjamin the Shepherd

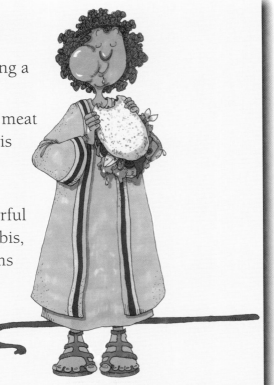

The rabbis of the Talmud got into a big debate over something a shepherd named Benjamin did.

Benjamin took a loaf of bread and cut it in half. He then put meat in the middle and began to eat and enjoy the sandwich. In his joy at eating his lunch, Benjamin called out, "This is a great sandwich. Praised be the God Who created it!"

Some of the rabbis thought that Benjamin had said a wonderful prayer, because it was based on true feelings. Two of the rabbis, Rabbi Yosi and Rav, thought that the prayer had big problems because Benjamin didn't use the same six words that begin most בְּרָכוֹת.

What do you think about Benjamin the shepherd's בְּרָכָה? Was it a good בְּרָכָה, or did it have problems?

The בְּרָכָה Formula

Here are a few more Hebrew words that you may already know that will help you translate the בְּרָכָה formula.

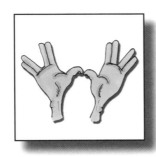

הָעוֹלָם   מֶלֶךְ   אַתָּה   בָּרוּךְ

The Eternal (God's Name) = יי

our God = אֱלֹהֵינוּ

בָּרוּךְ אַתָּה יי אֱלֹהֵינוּ מֶלֶךְ הָעוֹלָם

My own translation of the בְּרָכָה formula is:

God's Name

God has many different names. Each name teaches a different lesson about God. When we study prayers and blessings two names show up all the time. They are יי and אֱלֹהִים.

אֱלֹהִים is the Hebrew name for God. It is a job. We most often see the word אֱלֹהֵינוּ, which means "our God".

יי stands for God's actual name. That name is a secret. In ancient times only the High Priest in the Temple knew God's name. God's name was written יהוה but no one knew how to pronounce it correctly. So everyone else just said, אֲדֹנָי, "My Master" in its place. When we want to call God by name, we still use אֲדֹנָי. Most often it is written יי. This reminds us that we can never know everything about God.

Match the word to its picture.

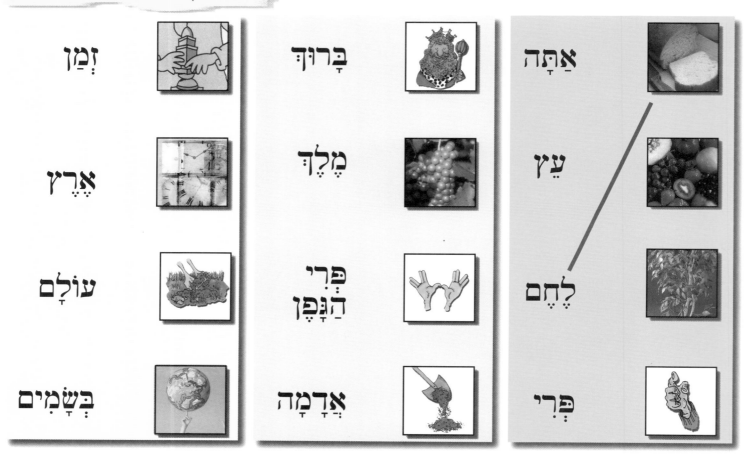

The Answer to Benjamin the Shepherd

A בְּרָכָה is said both for the person speaking it and for others who may be listening. A בְּרָכָה is both a way of thanking God and a way of teaching others about the things that God does. The problem with Benjamin's prayer is that when he said, "Praised be the God Who created it," he didn't name the God. People hearing it could fill in the name of their own pagan god. Or worse, they could think that Benjamin was praising himself for making the sandwich. After Benjamin, the Rabbis made it a rule that all בְּרָכוֹת should use these six words: בָּרוּךְ אַתָּה יי אֱלֹהֵינוּ מֶלֶךְ הָעוֹלָם. This formula names our God as the One God of the cosmos.

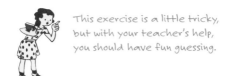

This exercise is a little tricky, but with your teacher's help, you should have fun guessing.

בְּרָכָה A Rebus

 Say and name these בְּרָכוֹת.

.1   יי אֱלֹהֵינוּ הַמּוֹצִיא

מִן **.**

.2   יי אֱלֹהֵינוּ בּוֹרֵא **.**

.3   יי אֱלֹהֵינוּ בּוֹרֵא מִינֵי    **.**

.4   יי אֱלֹהֵינוּ בּוֹרֵא    **.**

Match the blessing at the top with the actual words down below. Read them carefully.

‏3 _____ בּוֹרֵא מִינֵי מְזוֹנוֹת

_____ בּוֹרֵא פְּרִי הַגָּפֶן

_____ הַמּוֹצִיא לֶחֶם מִן הָאָרֶץ

_____ בּוֹרֵא פְּרִי הָעֵץ

עֲצֹר!

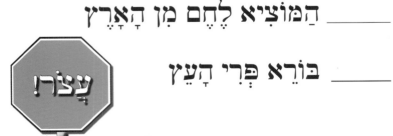

בְּרָכוֹת Over Foods and Aromas

Can you guess the purpose of each of these בְּרָכוֹת?

1. בָּרוּךְ אַתָּה יי אֱלֹהֵינוּ מֶלֶךְ הָעוֹלָם הַמּוֹצִיא לֶחֶם מִן הָאָרֶץ.

לֶחֶם

2. בָּרוּךְ אַתָּה יי אֱלֹהֵינוּ מֶלֶךְ הָעוֹלָם בּוֹרֵא פְּרִי הַגָּפֶן.

פְּרִי הַגֶּפֶן

3. בָּרוּךְ אַתָּה יי אֱלֹהֵינוּ מֶלֶךְ הָעוֹלָם בּוֹרֵא פְּרִי הָעֵץ.

4. בָּרוּךְ אַתָּה יי אֱלֹהֵינוּ מֶלֶךְ הָעוֹלָם בּוֹרֵא פְּרִי הָאֲדָמָה.

הָעֵץ

5. בָּרוּךְ אַתָּה יי אֱלֹהֵינוּ מֶלֶךְ הָעוֹלָם שֶׁהַכֹּל נִהְיֶה בִּדְבָרוֹ.

6. בָּרוּךְ אַתָּה יי אֱלֹהֵינוּ מֶלֶךְ הָעוֹלָם בּוֹרֵא מִינֵי מְזוֹנוֹת.

הָאֲדָמָה

7. בָּרוּךְ אַתָּה יי אֱלֹהֵינוּ מֶלֶךְ הָעוֹלָם בּוֹרֵא מִינֵי בְשָׂמִים.

כֹּל

all

The "The"

In English "pre" is a prefix. A prefix is something that comes at the beginning of a word and adds to its meaning. "Pre" means before.

הַ (or הָ) is a Hebrew prefix that means "the". When you add הַ to the word מוֹצִיא it becomes הַמּוֹצִיא, "the one who brings out", and when you add הָ to עֵץ, it becomes הָעֵץ, "the tree".

מְזוֹנוֹת

Underline the words below that have the "the"

8. עֵץ כֹּל הָעֵץ קָדוֹשׁ הָאָרֶץ הַמְבָרֵךְ מְבָרֵךְ

9. הָאֲדָמָה אֲדָמָה הָעוֹלָם אֶרֶץ הַכֹּל הָאֵל

בְשָׂמִים

11

Prayers Tell the Truth

_____Hamburger, Coke and Fries

_____Brownies

_____Sparkling Grape Juice

_____Two Eggs Over Easy, Hashbrowns and Toast

_____Fresh Raspberries

_____Pizza with Black Olives and Anchovies

_____Tofu

_____A Baked Tomato

The rabbis of the Talmud, the ones who shaped the prayers we now say, believed that it was really important for every prayer to tell the absolute truth. Here is the example they gave.

There is one בְּרָכָה we say over "fruit that grows from trees." There is another בְּרָכָה we say over "fruit that grows in the ground." In the Talmud they teach that it is okay if you say "the fruit from the ground" blessing over fruit that grows on a tree, because that בְּרָכָה is still a true statement. It is not okay to say "the fruit of the tree" blessing over things that grow on the ground. That is not a true statement. Fruit that grows on trees also grows in the ground, but fruit that grows in the ground does not grow on trees. Every time we say a בְּרָכָה it is our job to be a "witness" and "testify" to the things that God does.

To be a good witness, we must observe all the different things that God creates, and our testimony must always be true and accurate.

Maimonides, a famous Jewish teacher, wrote, "Anyone who eats any food or enjoys anything without saying a בְּרָכָה is a thief." What do you think he meant?

1. If a meal includes bread, you must say

בָּרוּךְ אַתָּה יי אֱלֹהֵינוּ מֶלֶךְ הָעוֹלָם
הַמּוֹצִיא לֶחֶם מִן הָאָרֶץ.

This blessing covers everything you will eat at that meal.

---

2. If there is no bread, but there is food made from flour, you say

בָּרוּךְ אַתָּה יי אֱלֹהֵינוּ מֶלֶךְ הָעוֹלָם
בּוֹרֵא מִינֵי מְזוֹנוֹת.

This blessing covers everything you will eat at that meal.

---

3. If there is wine (or grape juice), it gets its own blessing.

בָּרוּךְ אַתָּה יי אֱלֹהֵינוּ מֶלֶךְ הָעוֹלָם
בּוֹרֵא פְּרִי הַגָּפֶן.

---

4. If you are eating fruit that grows on trees, the blessing is

בָּרוּךְ אַתָּה יי אֱלֹהֵינוּ מֶלֶךְ הָעוֹלָם
בּוֹרֵא פְּרִי הָעֵץ.

---

5. If you are eating fruits or vegetables that grow in the ground, the blessing is

בָּרוּךְ אַתָּה יי אֱלֹהֵינוּ מֶלֶךְ הָעוֹלָם
בּוֹרֵא פְּרִי הָאֲדָמָה.

---

6. If you are eating many things, or if you are not sure what the food is made of, the "catch all" blessing is

בָּרוּךְ אַתָּה יי אֱלֹהֵינוּ מֶלֶךְ הָעוֹלָם
שֶׁהַכֹּל נִהְיֶה בִּדְבָרוֹ.

It thanks God for making everything.

עֲצֹר!

Write the number of the blessing that you would say over these meals.

_1_2_ Minestrone Soup with Crackers

_____ Turkey with Dressing, Peas, Mashed Potatoes and a Roll

_____ Orange Juice

The Answer to Maimonides

Maimonides began his book the Mishneh Torah by writing, "The basic principle of all principles, the foundation of all science, is knowing that One God created everything." Maimonides explains that our job is to examine the world and come to know and love the Creator through the creation. Our job is to appreciate everything that God created and thank God for it. When we fail to notice and learn, when we do not say thank you, we are "stealing" and not paying "the rent" on the things that God gave us.

13

בְּרָכוֹת Squares

Use this page to do a variety of tasks. Have students read across the rows. Call on a student to sound out the text in a particular box (for example, "Yosi, please read the text in גּ-שְׁתַּיִם"). Or play a game by asking students to assemble בְּרָכוֹת, pulling text from various boxes.

	ד	ג	ב	א
1 אַחַת	הָאֲדָמָה	אֱלֹהֵינוּ מֶלֶךְ הָעוֹלָם	הַזָּן אֶת הַכֹּל	לֶחֶם
2 שְׁתַּיִם	בְּשָׂמִים	בּוֹרֵא פְּרִי הַגָּפֶן	בָּרוּךְ אַתָּה יי אֱלֹהֵינוּ מֶלֶךְ הָעוֹלָם	נִהְיֶה בִּדְבָרוֹ
3 שָׁלֹשׁ	בּוֹרֵא פְּרִי	בּוֹרֵא	הָאָרֶץ	בּוֹרֵא מִינֵי
4 אַרְבַּע	מִן	הָעֵץ	שֶׁהַכֹּל	הַמּוֹצִיא
5 חָמֵשׁ	פְּרִי	מְזוֹנוֹת	בָּרוּךְ אַתָּה יי	הַגָּפֶן

Moses Sees the "Afterward" of God

The Torah tells us stories of times when people felt close to God. Jacob left home to escape his brother, who was really angry with him, and to find a wife. He camped at a place called Beth El and used a rock for a pillow. Jacob had an amazing dream in which a ladder rose from earth up into the heavens. Angels were going up the ladder and angels were coming down the ladder. Different people explain the meaning of this dream in different ways. When Jacob woke up he explained his dream by saying, "God was in this place, and I didn't realize it."

Moses also left home to escape being killed. On his journey he met his wife, Tziporah, and went to work as a shepherd for her father, Yitro. One day he led his flock far into the wilderness, to a mountain that would be known in the future as Sinai. There he had an experience of being close to God. Moses was awake when he saw a bush that burned and burned but did not burn up. God spoke to him out of this amazing bush, but Moses was afraid to look.

Years passed. Moses led the Jewish people back to that same mountain, Sinai. They heard God speak the Ten Commandments and then they ignored the commandments by making a golden calf. Moses had to go up the mountain for a second time to get a new Ten Commandments. While he was up there, he asked to be able to look at God. God told him, "No one can see

My face and live." Still, Moses asked again. So God told Moses to put his face into a crack in the rock. God put a hand over Moses to keep him from looking. God passed before Moses and then let him see the "afterward". Some people think that Moses saw God's back, but what the Hebrew really says is that Moses saw how things changed after God had been there. Moses saw the wake of God. A wake is the wave that appears after a boat goes by.

We are like Jacob and Moses. We want to get close to God, but that is not easy. We have to learn to realize that God is where we are—because we often forget that. And we have to learn that while we cannot see God, we can see God's "afterward". We can see the things God did. A בְּרָכָה is a way of saying that God is in this place. A בְּרָכָה is also a way of saying, "I noticed what God did, and I am thankful."

Questions

1. In what ways were Jacob and Moses alike?

2. How could Jacob not know that God was in a certain place if God was everywhere? Do you ever forget that God is where you are?

3. What things do you think Moses saw as part of God's "afterward"?

4. How can the stories of Jacob and Moses help you learn where to point your heart when you say a בְּרָכָה?

Understanding כַּוָּנָה

Saying a prayer with meaning is like trying to shoot an arrow into a target. The most important part of shooting an arrow is knowing how to aim. The same is true of praying. The Hebrew word we use for aiming is כַּוָּנָה. The rabbis teach that the secret to praying is to imagine God actually listening to your words. Prayers are like a ladder that goes from where you are to God. We "point our hearts" and climb up to God on our prayers. Each prayer has a story. Each story is a path we follow in our heart that leads us to God.

Practice these בְּרָכוֹת.

1. בָּרוּךְ אַתָּה יי אֱלֹהֵינוּ מֶלֶךְ הָעוֹלָם בּוֹרֵא פְּרִי הַגָּפֶן.

2. בָּרוּךְ אַתָּה יי אֱלֹהֵינוּ מֶלֶךְ הָעוֹלָם בּוֹרֵא פְּרִי הָעֵץ.

3. בָּרוּךְ אַתָּה יי אֱלֹהֵינוּ מֶלֶךְ הָעוֹלָם בּוֹרֵא מִינֵי בְשָׂמִים.

4. בָּרוּךְ אַתָּה יי אֱלֹהֵינוּ מֶלֶךְ הָעוֹלָם אֲשֶׁר קִדְּשָׁנוּ בְּמִצְוֹתָיו
וְצִוָּנוּ לִשְׁמוֹעַ קוֹל שׁוֹפָר.

5. בָּרוּךְ אַתָּה יי אֱלֹהֵינוּ מֶלֶךְ הָעוֹלָם בּוֹרֵא מִינֵי מְזוֹנוֹת.

6. בָּרוּךְ אַתָּה יי אֱלֹהֵינוּ מֶלֶךְ הָעוֹלָם אֲשֶׁר קִדְּשָׁנוּ בְּמִצְוֹתָיו
וְצִוָּנוּ לְהַדְלִיק נֵר שֶׁל שַׁבָּת.

7. בָּרוּךְ אַתָּה יי אֱלֹהֵינוּ מֶלֶךְ הָעוֹלָם הַמּוֹצִיא לֶחֶם מִן הָאָרֶץ.

8. בָּרוּךְ אַתָּה יי אֱלֹהֵינוּ מֶלֶךְ הָעוֹלָם אֲשֶׁר קִדְּשָׁנוּ בְּמִצְוֹתָיו
וְצִוָּנוּ עַל אֲכִילַת מַצָּה.

Circle the words with the "the" at the beginning.

9. שְׁמַע הָאָרֶץ כֹּל הָעֵץ עֵץ הַגָּפֶן הָעוֹלָם עוֹלָם

10. הָאֵלֶּה כֹּל אֲדָמָה הַקָּדוֹשׁ הַמְּלָכִים גֶּפֶן הַמְבֹרָךְ

11. אֶרֶץ הַשַּׁבָּת הַכֹּל הָאֲדָמָה אֶרֶץ הַמּוֹצִיא מוֹצִיא

A Review

Some things to Know about בְּרָכוֹת

- A בְּרָכָה is a prayer that starts or ends with a formula that uses the word בָּרוּךְ.

- בְּרָכוֹת use a formula, usually: בָּרוּךְ אַתָּה יי אֱלֹהֵינוּ מֶלֶךְ הָעוֹלָם

- בְּרָכוֹת are said at many different times. Some בְּרָכוֹת are said over eating.

- Different foods take different בְּרָכוֹת because בְּרָכוֹת must tell the truth. We cannot use the same בְּרָכָה over something that grows in the ground as we use over something that grows on a tree.

- בְּרָכוֹת are ways of thanking God. They are also tools for learning how to be like God. But most importantly, בְּרָכוֹת are ways of getting close to God because they help us to notice the things that God does.

בְּרָכוֹת Words

Some of the words we learned or reviewed in this lesson are:

בְּשָׂמִים   עֵץ   הָעוֹלָם   מֶלֶךְ   אֱלֹהֵינוּ   יי   אַתָּה   בָּרוּךְ

פֵּירוֹת   פְּרִי הַגֶּפֶן   לֶחֶם

בְּרָכוֹת we have learned:

בָּרוּךְ אַתָּה יי אֱלֹהֵינוּ מֶלֶךְ הָעוֹלָם הַמּוֹצִיא לֶחֶם מִן הָאָרֶץ.

בָּרוּךְ אַתָּה יי אֱלֹהֵינוּ מֶלֶךְ הָעוֹלָם בּוֹרֵא פְּרִי הַגֶּפֶן.

בָּרוּךְ אַתָּה יי אֱלֹהֵינוּ מֶלֶךְ הָעוֹלָם בּוֹרֵא פְּרִי הָעֵץ.

בָּרוּךְ אַתָּה יי אֱלֹהֵינוּ מֶלֶךְ הָעוֹלָם בּוֹרֵא פְּרִי הָאֲדָמָה.

בָּרוּךְ אַתָּה יי אֱלֹהֵינוּ מֶלֶךְ הָעוֹלָם שֶׁהַכֹּל נִהְיֶה בִּדְבָרוֹ.

בָּרוּךְ אַתָּה יי אֱלֹהֵינוּ מֶלֶךְ הָעוֹלָם בּוֹרֵא מִינֵי מְזוֹנוֹת.

בָּרוּךְ אַתָּה יי אֱלֹהֵינוּ מֶלֶךְ הָעוֹלָם בּוֹרֵא מִינֵי בְשָׂמִים.

עֲצֹר!

בְּרְכוֹת מִצְוָה

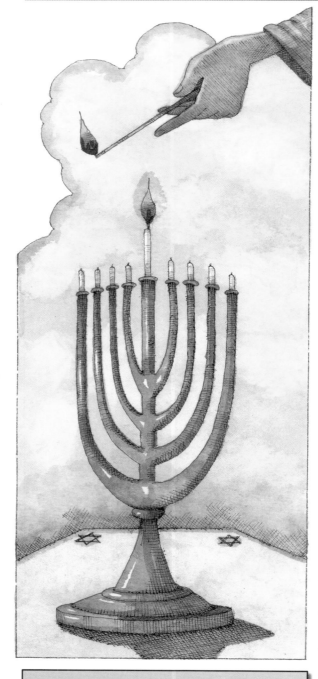

Being a Jew means trying to:

- learn about and love God,
- become the best person we can be,
- make the world into the best possible place for everyone.

The Torah is the guidebook that God gave the Jewish people. When you study the Torah, you learn that it tells us 613 rules for living that bring us close to God and help us to live the way God wants us to live.

Some of these rules are about holiday celebrations like Passover, Sukkot, and Shabbat. Some of them are good things to do like loving your neighbor, giving tzedakah, and helping people to get well. And some of the rules are about things we should not to do. These include not murdering or embarrassing another person, and not hating another person in our heart.

We call these ways of living, מִצְוֹת. They are things that God told us to do and things that God told us not to do.

Some (but not all) מִצְוֹת have בְּרָכוֹת. These בְּרָכוֹת help us to remember that the reason we are doing these things is to get closer to God. There is a בְּרָכָה for putting on a tallit, lighting candles, studying Torah, and sitting in a sukkah.

A מִצְוָה blessing is different from an ordinary בְּרָכָה. We add a few more words to the beginning. We add

אֲשֶׁר קִדְּשָׁנוּ בְּמִצְוֹתָיו וְצִוָּנוּ

This blessing formula says that when we do a מִצְוָה we make a connection to the holy. This בְּרָכָה with extra words reminds us that the thing we are doing is a chance to experience holiness.

In this unit you will learn
- about מִצְוֹת
- seven בְּרָכוֹת we say when we do מִצְוֹת
- three Hebrew roots
- one story about מִצְוֹת.

19

בִּרְכוֹת מִצְוָה

Use these words to guess the purpose of each בְּרָכָה.

שׁוֹפָר

לוּלָב

מְזוּזָה

1. בָּרוּךְ אַתָּה יי אֱלֹהֵינוּ מֶלֶךְ הָעוֹלָם אֲשֶׁר קִדְּשָׁנוּ בְּמִצְוֹתָיו וְצִוָּנוּ עַל מִקְרָא מְגִלָּה.

2. בָּרוּךְ אַתָּה יי אֱלֹהֵינוּ מֶלֶךְ הָעוֹלָם אֲשֶׁר קִדְּשָׁנוּ בְּמִצְוֹתָיו וְצִוָּנוּ לְהַדְלִיק נֵר שֶׁל שַׁבָּת.

3. בָּרוּךְ אַתָּה יי אֱלֹהֵינוּ מֶלֶךְ הָעוֹלָם אֲשֶׁר קִדְּשָׁנוּ בְּמִצְוֹתָיו וְצִוָּנוּ עַל אֲכִילַת מַצָּה.

טַלִּית

4. בָּרוּךְ אַתָּה יי אֱלֹהֵינוּ מֶלֶךְ הָעוֹלָם אֲשֶׁר קִדְּשָׁנוּ בְּמִצְוֹתָיו וְצִוָּנוּ לִשְׁמוֹעַ קוֹל שׁוֹפָר.

שַׁבָּת

5. בָּרוּךְ אַתָּה יי אֱלֹהֵינוּ מֶלֶךְ הָעוֹלָם אֲשֶׁר קִדְּשָׁנוּ בְּמִצְוֹתָיו וְצִוָּנוּ לְהַדְלִיק נֵר שֶׁל חֲנֻכָּה.

6. בָּרוּךְ אַתָּה יי אֱלֹהֵינוּ מֶלֶךְ הָעוֹלָם אֲשֶׁר קִדְּשָׁנוּ בְּמִצְוֹתָיו וְצִוָּנוּ לִקְבֹּעַ מְזוּזָה.

חֲנֻכָּה

7. בָּרוּךְ אַתָּה יי אֱלֹהֵינוּ מֶלֶךְ הָעוֹלָם אֲשֶׁר קִדְּשָׁנוּ בְּמִצְוֹתָיו וְצִוָּנוּ לְהִתְעַטֵּף בַּצִּיצִית.

מַצָּה

8. בָּרוּךְ אַתָּה יי אֱלֹהֵינוּ מֶלֶךְ הָעוֹלָם אֲשֶׁר קִדְּשָׁנוּ בְּמִצְוֹתָיו וְצִוָּנוּ עַל נְטִילַת לוּלָב.

What can be learned from the last word or two of a בְּרָכָה?

מְגִלָּה

Roots are the secret to understanding what Hebrew means. מלך is a root.

Can you see the three letters מלך in these words?

מַלְכֵנוּ יִמְלֹךְ מַלְכוּתוֹ

Hebrew builds words out of three-letter roots.

our king = מַלְכֵנוּ

He will rule = יִמְלֹךְ

His kingdom = מַלְכוּתוֹ

CLUE: כ = כ = ך

Hebrew often uses male words to talk about God, but that does not mean that God is male.

Sound out these words and circle those that contain the root מלך.

1. אֶחָד מַלְכוּתוֹ כְּבוֹד בָּרְכוּ מֶלֶךְ מַלְכֵי

2. הַמְּלָכִים וָעֶד שְׁמַע הַמְבֹרָךְ מַלְכֵנוּ בָּרֵךְ

3. אֶת יי שֵׁם כְּבוֹד אֵין כֵּאלֹהֵנוּ מַלְכֵנוּ

4. בָּרוּךְ אַתָּה מֶלֶךְ הָעוֹלָם אֲשֶׁר קִדְּשָׁנוּ

5. כְּמַלְכֵנוּ אֵין כְּמוֹשִׁיעֵנוּ מַלְכוּתְךָ בְּמִצְוֹתָיו

Write in the missing letters of the root word מלך.

6. כְּמַ__כֵּנוּ

7. מַלְ__וּתוֹ

8. __לְכֵי

9. מֶלֶ__

10. מַ__כוּתְךָ

11. הַ__לָכִים

21

Practice these בְּרָכָה words.

1. בָּרוּךְ שַׁבָּת נֵר עַל אֲשֶׁר קִדְּשָׁנוּ לוּלָב

2. מְגִלָּה מַצָּה אַתָּה יי שֶׁל חֲנֻכָּה וְצִוָּנוּ

3. עַל אֲכִילַת צִיצִת לִשְׁמוֹעַ קוֹל מְזוּזָה

4. מִקְרָא בְּמִצְוֹתָיו לְהַדְלִיק לִקְבֹּעַ נְטִילַת

5. לְהִתְעַטֵּף אֱלֹהֵינוּ קִדְּשָׁנוּ הַמּוֹצִיא לֶחֶם פְּרִי

Recite these בְּרָכָה phrases.

6. בָּרוּךְ אַתָּה יי אֱלֹהֵינוּ מֶלֶךְ   אֲשֶׁר קִדְּשָׁנוּ בְּמִצְוֹתָיו

7. וְצִוָּנוּ לְהַדְלִיק נֵר שֶׁל שַׁבָּת   וְצִוָּנוּ לִשְׁמוֹעַ קוֹל שׁוֹפָר

8. וְצִוָּנוּ עַל אֲכִילַת מַצָּה   וְצִוָּנוּ עַל נְטִילַת לוּלָב

9. וְצִוָּנוּ עַל מִקְרָא מְגִלָּה   וְצִוָּנוּ לִקְבֹּעַ מְזוּזָה

Recite this בְּרָכָה.

10. בָּרוּךְ אַתָּה יי אֱלֹהֵינוּ מֶלֶךְ הָעוֹלָם אֲשֶׁר קִדְּשָׁנוּ בְּמִצְוֹתָיו
וְצִוָּנוּ לְהַדְלִיק נֵר שֶׁל חֲנֻכָּה.

The מִצְוָה of Lighting

Most Jewish holidays begin twice, once when the candles are lit and blessed and then again when the קִדּוּשׁ is said over the wine. Both of these בְּרָכוֹת help us recognize the holiness of Shabbat or the festival and make the holiness part of our experience.

Kindling (lighting) candles to mark the beginning of Shabbat or a festival and lighting the Ḥanukkah lights are מִצְוֹת. Each of these acts of lighting a flame is an opportunity—a chance to kindle a feeling of holiness inside ourselves.

1. בָּרוּךְ אַתָּה יי אֱלֹהֵינוּ מֶלֶךְ הָעוֹלָם

2. אֲשֶׁר קִדְּשָׁנוּ בְּמִצְוֹתָיו וְצִוָּנוּ

3. לְהַדְלִיק נֵר שֶׁל שַׁבָּת.

4. בָּרוּךְ אַתָּה יי אֱלֹהֵינוּ מֶלֶךְ הָעוֹלָם

5. אֲשֶׁר קִדְּשָׁנוּ בְּמִצְוֹתָיו וְצִוָּנוּ

6. לְהַדְלִיק נֵר שֶׁל חֲנֻכָּה.

7. בָּרוּךְ אַתָּה יי אֱלֹהֵינוּ מֶלֶךְ הָעוֹלָם

8. אֲשֶׁר קִדְּשָׁנוּ בְּמִצְוֹתָיו וְצִוָּנוּ

9. לְהַדְלִיק נֵר שֶׁל יוֹם טוֹב.

My own translation of this part of the בְּרָכָה:

לְהַדְלִיק נֵר שֶׁל שַׁבָּת

Can you see these letters צוה in these words?

בְּמִצְוֹתָיו וְצִוָּנוּ מִצְוָה

Sometimes the letter ה drops out in words.

The root צוה means "command".

commandment = מִצְוָה

and commanded us = וְצִוָּנוּ

with God's commandments = בְּמִצְוֹתָיו

Practice these words and circle all that contain the root צוה.

1.	מִצְוֹת מֶלֶךְ מוֹשִׁיעֵנוּ קָדוֹשׁ צִוָּה לָנוּ
2.	בְּרוּכִים הַבָּאִים מִצְוָה תוֹרָה אֲשֶׁר קִדְּשָׁנוּ
3.	שְׁמַע יִשְׂרָאֵל שָׁלוֹם קְדוּשָׁה מִצְוֹה מַלְכֵּנוּ
4.	וְצִוָּנוּ הָעֵץ הַגֶּפֶן מַלְכוּתוֹ מְזוֹנוֹת צַו
5.	לְהַדְלִיק צִוָּה מִצְוֹת שׁוֹמֵעַ מְגִלָּה קָדוֹשׁ

Write in the missing letters for these words built from the roots צוה and מלך.

6. מִצְ__ָה

7. מַלְ__וּתוֹ

8. וְ__ִ__נוּ

9. __מֶלֶ__

10. צַ__

11. הַ__ִ__לָכִים

24

Endings also give us a lot of information. נוּ is the first ending we are going to learn.

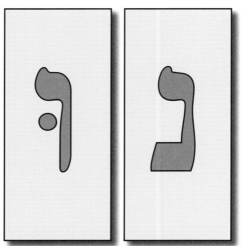

Can you see the two letters נוּ in these words?

אֲבוֹתֵינוּ   אֱלֹהֵינוּ   מַלְכֵּנוּ

נוּ means "our" or "us".

our Ruler = מַלְכֵּנוּ

our God = אֱלֹהֵינוּ

our ancestors = אֲבוֹתֵינוּ

Sound and circle the words that end in נוּ.

1. מַלְכֵּנוּ   אָבִינוּ   אָבוֹת   אֲדָמָה   עֵינֵינוּ   בָּרְכוּ

2. שְׁמַע   הַמְבֹרָךְ   כְּמוֹשִׁיעֵנוּ   בָּרְכֵנוּ   עָלֵינוּ

3. פָּנֶיךָ   כֻּלָנוּ   אֲנַחְנוּ   וְאִמוֹתֵינוּ   כָּתְבֵנוּ

אֵין כֵּאלֹהֵינוּ

These words come from an ancient hymn of praise to God. For more than 1500 years it has been sung at the end of morning services on Shabbat and holidays.

מוֹשִׁיעַ	מֶלֶךְ	אָדוֹן	אֱלֹהִים
4. אֵין כְּמוֹשִׁיעֵנוּ	אֵין כְּמַלְכֵּנוּ	אֵין כַּאדוֹנֵינוּ	אֵין כֵּאלֹהֵינוּ
5. מִי כְמוֹשִׁיעֵנוּ	מִי כְמַלְכֵּנוּ	מִי כַאדוֹנֵינוּ	מִי כֵאלֹהֵינוּ
6. נוֹדֶה לְמוֹשִׁיעֵנוּ	נוֹדֶה לְמַלְכֵּנוּ	נוֹדֶה לַאדוֹנֵינוּ	נוֹדֶה לֵאלֹהֵינוּ
7. בָּרוּךְ מוֹשִׁיעֵנוּ	בָּרוּךְ מַלְכֵּנוּ	בָּרוּךְ אֲדוֹנֵינוּ	בָּרוּךְ אֱלֹהֵינוּ
8. אַתָּה הוּא מוֹשִׁיעֵנוּ	אַתָּה הוּא מַלְכֵּנוּ	אַתָּה הוּא אֲדוֹנֵינוּ	אַתָּה הוּא אֱלֹהֵינוּ

The History of מִצְוֹת

מִצְוֹת are things that God wants us to do and things that God wants us not to do. When Adam and Eve left the Garden of Eden, God gave them one rule.* This מִצְוָה was "No Idols." That didn't really mean Adam and Even shouldn't carve figures out of wood and stone. It really meant, "Remember that there is only one God." Never think that you can be God, and never think that you can make up a god who will give you permission to do things you want to do (when you know they are wrong).

The "No Idols" rule didn't work. People's feelings won out over the things they knew were right. People stole. People hit and even killed. People made fun of each other. They did what they felt like doing and forgot that one God created everyone.

After the flood, God made a new start. God taught Noah and his family six more מִצְוֹת. God kept the (1) "No Idols" מִצְוָה and added these מִצְוֹת: (2) be good to your family, (3) no murder, (4) no stealing, (5) no cursing out God, (6) no being cruel to animals, and (7) set up courts to fix things when you are angry at each other. God hoped that if the rules were more specific people would act better. It didn't work. Even with seven מִצְוֹת people still hurt, killed, stole, and more or less did what they wanted. The world wasn't much better.

---

*There were actually two other rules, but "be fruitful and multiply" doesn't count because it was given to all life, and not just to people. And "don't eat the fruit from the tree in the middle of the garden" doesn't count because it was particular to the people living in the garden. God only gave Adam and Eve one מִצְוָה that is still on the list.

The next time, God went for an experiment. God picked one family, Abram's family, and said, "We are going to make a deal. I will work with you, and when we figure out the rules, you will teach everyone else." So God gave the Families-of-Israel lots of rules, 613 מִצְוֹת. Israel got the Torah with holidays and stories, things to do every day, and a large collections of "Do This" or "Don't Do This" rules. God gave Abram's family the gift of not just a couple of rules but a whole way of living. God hoped that the Torah would help them to make themselves into better people—and help them teach others how to be better people, too.

It is hard to be a Jew. Torah comes with a lot of rules about things to do and not to do. But being a Jew also offers a path to happiness by letting the best "you" emerge and join with others to make a much better world.

From the Midrash

Question

What is the point of the מִצְוֹת? Why did God give them to us?

Answer to מִצְוֹת

The Torah is a gift from God. It contains 613 מִצְוֹת. 248 of them are positive מִצְוֹת. These are things that God wants us to "do." 365 of them are negative. These are things that God wants us to "not do."

There are 248 bones in a human body. That means that מִצְוֹת are supposed to shape the things we do and not do.

There are 365 days in the year. We are supposed to let the מִצְוֹת guide what we do and what we do not do every day.

The big idea is this: everything we do, every day, comes with a chance to know God better. We always have the chance to become better people and to work together to make the world better, too.

Here are a few more Hebrew words that you may already know.

Please make your best guess. Your teacher will help you twist roots into words.

מִצְוָה

mitzvah
commandment

קָדוֹשׁ

holy

אֲשֶׁר

who/that/
which

My own translation of this בְּרָכָה formula is:

אֲשֶׁר קִדְּשָׁנוּ בְּמִצְוֹתָיו וְצִוָּנוּ

עֲצֹר!

_____

Can you see the three letters קדש in these words?

קָדוֹשׁ　　מְקַדֵּשׁ　　קִדְּשָׁנוּ

קדש means "holy".

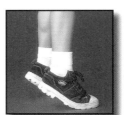

holy = קָדוֹשׁ

makes holy = מְקַדֵּשׁ

makes us holy = קִדְּשָׁנוּ

Practice these words and circle each one that contains the root קדש.

1. אֲשֶׁר　וְצִוָּנוּ　קִדְּשָׁנוּ　הַקָּדוֹשׁ　בָּרוּךְ　הוּא

2. לְהִתְעַטֵּף　מִצְוָה　מִקְרָא　מְקַדֵּשׁ　לִקְבֹּעַ　פְּרִי

3. עַל　אֲכִילַת　צִיצִית　לִשְׁמֹעַ　קוֹל　מְזוּזָה

4. מִקְרָא　בְּמִצְוֹתָיו　לְהַדְלִיק　לִקְבֹּעַ　נְטִילַת

5. אֱלֹהֵינוּ　קִדְּשָׁנוּ　פְּרִי　הַמּוֹצִיא　לֶחֶם　לְהִתְעַטֵּף

Write in the missing letters for these words that are built from the root קדש.

6. קָ__וֹשׁ　　7. __ְ__ֻדָּשָׁה　　8. מְקַדֵּ__

9. קִ__ְשָׁנוּ　　10. בִּקְדוּ__ָתוֹ　　11. __ַ__ֵּשׁ

29

Practice these בְּרָכָה words. Circle words made from צוה , underline those from קדשׁ, and draw a box around מלך words.

1. הַגָּפֶן שׁוֹפָר קִדְּשָׁנוּ אֲדָמָה מַלְכוּתוֹ נְטִילַת צִוָּה

2. בּוֹרֵא פֵּירוֹת קוֹל לֶחֶם אֲכִילַת וְצִוָּנוּ לְמַלְכֵּנוּ

3. מְזוּזָה חֲנֻכָּה מִן שַׁבָּת לִקְבֹּעַ אֱלֹהֵינוּ מוֹשִׁיעֵנוּ

4. בָּרוּךְ אַתָּה מֶלֶךְ נוֹדֶה קָדוֹשׁ קְדוּשָׁה בְּמִצְוֹתָיו

Practice these בְּרָכוֹת phrases.

5. לְהַדְלִיק נֵר שֶׁל שַׁבָּת   נֵר שֶׁל חֲנֻכָּה   נֵר שֶׁל יוֹם טוֹב

6. בּוֹרֵא מִינֵי מְזוֹנוֹת   בּוֹרֵא פְּרִי הָעֵץ   בּוֹרֵא פְּרִי הַגָּפֶן

7. שֶׁהַכֹּל נִהְיֶה בִּדְבָרוֹ   בּוֹרֵא מִינֵי מְזוֹנוֹת   אֲשֶׁר קִדְּשָׁנוּ

Recite these בְּרָכוֹת (begin each with line 8).

8. בָּרוּךְ אַתָּה יי אֱלֹהֵינוּ מֶלֶךְ הָעוֹלָם...

9. אֲשֶׁר קִדְּשָׁנוּ בְּמִצְוֹתָיו וְצִוָּנוּ עַל אֲכִילַת מַצָּה

10. אֲשֶׁר קִדְּשָׁנוּ בְּמִצְוֹתָיו וְצִוָּנוּ לִשְׁמוֹעַ קוֹל שׁוֹפָר

11. אֲשֶׁר קִדְּשָׁנוּ בְּמִצְוֹתָיו וְצִוָּנוּ עַל מִקְרָא מְגִלָּה

30

The Flying Letters

This is a story of two towns. One was rich and one was poor. The rich town had a large, beautiful synagogue that was almost always closed. The small town had a room in the back of a store that they used for their synagogue. But people came every day and the place was always full. The rich synagogue had a *Sefer Torah* that was opened only a few times a year. The poor synagogue had an empty scroll of parchment stretched between two wooden rollers that they kept in the ark. They hoped someday to have the money to pay a scribe to fill it with Hebrew letters and words—to write down the Torah on it. Meanwhile, whenever they had to read Torah they took out their empty scroll and read the holy words from a book.

People in the two towns were very different. In the poor town, everyone thought of their neighbors as their family. In the rich town, people took care of themselves. In the one town, sick people had to fend for themselves. In the other town, if you were sick, lots of people brought you chicken soup. In one town, mourners were left alone to be sad. In the other town, if someone died, lots of people stopped by to comfort those who mourned. In the one town, people lived their lives pretty much alone. In the other town people shared one another's joy and sadness.

One night, just before Rosh ha-Shanah, the Torah reader of the rich synagogue opened the building to make sure that the Torah was rolled to the right place. The synagogue was dark and quiet. When he opened the ark door, hundreds of Hebrew letters flew out of the ark and surrounded him. It was like being attacked by a swarm of bees. He brushed them away and shut the ark door. He ran home and forgot to lock the synagogue door. He didn't tell anyone what had happened. He was sure he had dreamt it.

That same night some men from the poor town were walking home from evening prayers. They looked at the sliver of the moon and were sure that they saw a swarm of Hebrew letters fly across its face looking like a swarm of bats. But they told each other, "It must have been bats, because Hebrew letters don't fly."

On Rosh ha-Shanah, the congregation of the rich town took out their *Sefer Torah* and opened it to begin to read. They had a big shock. Their scroll was empty. No words. No letters. All of the Torah was now missing from their scroll.

At the same moment, the families of the poor town had a shock. When they opened their empty scroll to pretend to read, they found it filled with words and letters. It had become a complete Torah.

From a story by David Einhorn

Questions

1. Why did the rich community lose the words in its Torah?
2. Why did the poor community get words in its Torah?
3. What is the meaning of this story?
4. How can this story of the flying letters help you learn where to point your heart when you say a בְּרָכָה?

Your teacher may want you to try this at home.

The words to these **בְּרָכוֹת** are flying from one synagogue to another. Connect them to make as many **בְּרָכוֹת** as possible. (Parts can be used as many times as you want.)

בָּרוּךְ אַתָּה יי

אֱלֹהֵינוּ מֶלֶךְ הָעוֹלָם

אֲשֶׁר קִדְּשָׁנוּ בְּמִצְוֹתָיו וְצִוָּנוּ

לְהַדְלִיק נֵר שֶׁל שַׁבָּת

בּוֹרֵא מִינֵי מְזוֹנוֹת

הַמּוֹצִיא לֶחֶם מִן הָאָרֶץ

לִקְבֹּעַ מְזוּזָה

עַל נְטִילַת לוּלָב

בּוֹרֵא פְּרִי הָעֵץ

בּוֹרֵא פְּרִי הַגָּפֶן

לִשְׁמוֹעַ קוֹל שׁוֹפָר

33

A Review

Some things to Know about בִּרְכוֹת מִצְוָה

- מִצְוֹת are found in the Torah. They are things to do and things not to do, and they give us the chance to learn about and love God, become the best person we can be, and make the world the best possible place.

- There are בְּרָכוֹת to say when doing some מִצְוֹת. Not all מִצְוֹת have בְּרָכוֹת.

- When we say a בְּרָכָה over a מִצְוָה we add these words to the בְּרָכָה formula:
  אֲשֶׁר קִדְּשָׁנוּ בְּמִצְוֹתָיו וְצִוָּנוּ

Language Learning

We learned or reviewed the following words:

מְגִלָּה   מַצָּה   חֲנֻכָּה   שַׁבָּת   טַלִית   מְזוּזָה   לוּלָב   שׁוֹפָר

טוֹב   יוֹם   of   נֵר   לְהַדְלִיק

We looked at the following roots: צ ו ה , מ ל ך , ק ד שׁ ,

and the suffix נ וּ .

We learned the following בְּרָכוֹת

בָּרוּךְ אַתָּה יי אֱלֹהֵינוּ מֶלֶךְ הָעוֹלָם אֲשֶׁר קִדְּשָׁנוּ בְּמִצְוֹתָיו וְצִוָּנוּ...

...עַל מִקְרָא מְגִלָּה.   ...לְהַדְלִיק נֵר שֶׁל יוֹם טוֹב.   ...לְהִתְעַטֵּף בַּצִּיצִית.

...לְהַדְלִיק נֵר שֶׁל שַׁבָּת.   ...עַל אֲכִילַת מַצָּה.   ...עַל נְטִילַת לוּלָב.

...לְהַדְלִיק נֵר שֶׁל חֲנֻכָּה.   ...לִשְׁמוֹעַ קוֹל שׁוֹפָר.   ...לִקְבֹּעַ מְזוּזָה.

עֲצֹר!

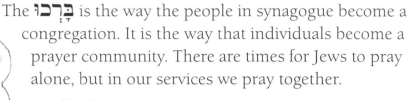

The בָּרְכוּ

The בָּרְכוּ is the way the people in synagogue become a congregation. It is the way that individuals become a prayer community. There are times for Jews to pray alone, but in our services we pray together.

The בָּרְכוּ is an invitation. It is a call and response. That means that the prayer leader asks a question and the congregation answers together. In answering it becomes a community.

The leader asks: בָּרְכוּ אֶת־יי הַמְבֹרָךְ

Are you ready to say "בְּרָכוֹת" to יי?

When everyone says,

בָּרוּךְ יי הַמְבֹרָךְ לְעוֹלָם וָעֶד

the congregation is created and the community is formed. The answer means:

Yes, God deserves בְּרָכוֹת forever and always.

This pattern of call and response as an invitation is used two other times in Jewish life.

The exact same words are used to begin the blessings before the reading of the Torah. And very similar words (and the same pattern) are used to begin *Birkat ha-Mazon*, the blessing after eating that is said only when a community (at least three people) eats together.

Why do you think these three events—praying, reading Torah, and the end of a meal—require a special way of forming community?

The בָּרְכוּ is said only if there is a minyan, a group of at least ten people praying together.

In this unit you will learn
- about the בָּרְכוּ
- the Hebrew root ברך
- two stories about the בָּרְכוּ.

35

This root is found in every בְּרָכָה.

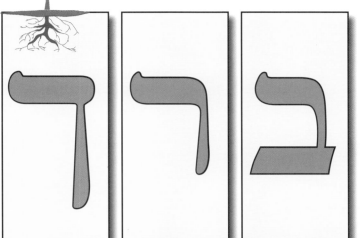

Can you see the three letters בּרכ in these words?

הַמְבֹרָךְ   בָּרְכוּ   בָּרוּךְ

Hebrew builds words out of three-letter roots.

bless = בָּרוּךְ

bless (plural) = בָּרְכוּ

the One who is blessed = הַמְבֹרָךְ

CLUE: בּ = כּ = ךְ

Practice these words and circle all the words that contain the root בּרכ.

1. מַלְכֵי   מֶלֶךְ   בָּרְכוּ   כְּבוֹד   מַלְכוּתוֹ   בָּרוּךְ

2. בָּרֵךְ   מַלְכֵנוּ   הַמְבֹרָךְ   שְׁמַע   וָעֶד   הַמְּלָכִים

3. לִבְרָכָה   בָּרָא   בְּרוּכִים   אֵין   מְבָרֵךְ   כְּבוֹד

4. בָּרְכוּנִי   הָעוֹלָם   מֶלֶךְ   בִּרְכַּת   אַתָּה   בָּרוּךְ

5. בְּמִצְוֹתָיו   בָּרְכֵנוּ   בְּרָכוֹת   אֵין   כְּמַלְכֵנוּ

Write in the missing root letters.

6. בָּרוּ___

7. הַמְ___רָךְ

8. בָּרְ___וּ

9. בְּ___כַּת

10. בְּרָ___וֹת

11. ___רוּכִים

36

The First בָּרְכוּ

All Jews used to gather on a mountain in Jerusalem to worship and come close to God. Three times a year everyone would go to the Temple. At those times, Jews felt like they really belonged, and at those moments God felt very close. Then it was over. The Babylonians conquered Jerusalem, and the Temple was destroyed and left in ruins. The Jews were carried away as slaves, and the mountain where the Jews had gathered was empty. Israel was in exile.

It took seventy years to get permission to return. At first, only a few Jews left their new homes and their new businesses to become pioneers. They began to rebuild the Land of Israel and rebuild the Temple, but it did not go well. There were many problems. Finally, two new leaders came from Babylonia. They were Ezra and Nehemiah. To bring people together they held an eight-day festival in the center of the unfinished Temple courtyard. For three of those days, for the first time ever, the Torah was read from beginning to end.

At the beginning of this gathering, when everyone was standing in the unfinished courtyard waiting to see what would happen, the Levites got up on the stage. The Levites were the singers and musicians who led services in the Temple. They broke the silence with words that were more or less the בָּרְכוּ. The people answered with their part. When this בָּרְכוּ ended, the exile was over. Israel was again one people, and they again had a home.

From the Hirsch Commentary on the Siddur

Questions
1. How did saying the בָּרְכוּ end the exile?
2. How can remembering this first בָּרְכוּ in the unfinished Temple help us to know where to point our hearts when we say the בָּרְכוּ?

Practice reciting these phrases that contain the root בּרך.

1. בָּרוּךְ אַתָּה יי אֱלֹהֵינוּ מֶלֶךְ הָעוֹלָם בּוֹרֵא פְּרִי הַגָּפֶן.

2. בָּרְכוּ אֶת-יי הַמְבֹרָךְ. בָּרוּךְ יי הַמְבֹרָךְ לְעוֹלָם וָעֶד.

3. בָּרְכוּנִי לְשָׁלוֹם מַלְאֲכֵי הַשָּׁלוֹם מַלְאֲכֵי עֶלְיוֹן.

4. מִי שֶׁבֵּרַךְ אֲבוֹתֵינוּ אַבְרָהָם יִצְחָק וְיַעֲקֹב, שָׂרָה רִבְקָה רָחֵל וְלֵאָה.

5. יִתְבָּרַךְ וְיִשְׁתַּבַּח וְיִתְפָּאַר וְיִתְרוֹמַם וְיִתְנַשֵּׂא וְיִתְהַדָּר וְיִתְעַלֶּה וְיִתְהַלָּל.

Being a Community

The בָּרְכוּ turns the group of people who have come to a service into a community.

List three groups to which you belong.

1. _____
2. _____
3. _____

List three communities to which you belong.

1. _____
2. _____
3. _____

What is the difference between a group and a community?

38

בָּרְכוּ אֶת-יי הַמְבֹרָךְ

אֶת-יי

What is your best guess about what the first line means?

Take your best guess at these meanings. Your teacher will help you fill in the parts you don't yet know.

Adonai = יי

and more = וָעֶד

before direct object = אֶת

to = לְ

the = הַ

בָּרוּךְ יי הַמְבֹרָךְ לְעוֹלָם וָעֶד.

וָעֶד. לְ יי

What is your best guess about what the second line means?

How to dance the בָּרְכוּ

We say the בָּרְכוּ with our bodies as well as with our mouths.

Take a breath and let it out slowly. It should make you feel alive. A good breath goes through your whole body. In Hebrew, one word for breath is connected to the word for soul. In Genesis we learned that we come alive when God breathes our soul into our body. The first secret to saying the בָּרְכוּ is breathing and feeling the breath run through your body, reminding you of the gift of life.

The second secret to saying the בָּרְכוּ is knowing that the Hebrew root ברך is also the word for knees. We bow when we say the בָּרְכוּ. We bow deeply, just like a person who is entering a room where a king or queen is waiting. We bow by first bending our knees and then bending our spine.

The last secret to saying the בָּרְכוּ is remembering that it is a call and response. We stand while the leader bows and says the first line, "בָּרְכוּ." We bend and bow when we say our line, "בָּרוּךְ יי." We breathe out as we bend our knees and bow. We breathe back in as we come back up—unbending and unbowing.

The Power of a Minyan

The midrash teaches that Abraham figured out that ten was the smallest number of people to make sure that prayers had a good chance of convincing God. Abraham realized this when he was trying to save Sodom. He argued with God that it was wrong to destroy Sodom if enough righteous people lived there. God agreed not to destroy the city if there were fifty good people. Then Abraham tried smaller numbers and stopped at ten. We've used ten ever since. Ten or more Jews praying together are a minyan. The Hasidim understood the power of a minyan and told this story.

There was a blind rebbe who was called the Seer of Lublin. The Seer could not see things through his eyes but he saw in other ways. One of the students of the Seer was a man who lived in a town where there were no other Jews. One week a year the student would leave his farm, ride almost two days on his horse, and then spend a week studying with, praying with, and being part of the Seer's community.

Once he rode into Lublin late on a Thursday afternoon. He went to put his horse away in the stable and found the Seer waiting for him. Almost magically, the blind Seer called him by name and said, "Go home."

The man said, "But—"

The Seer said, "Go home and get there before Shabbat starts."

The man said, "But it is Thursday afternoon, and my farm is two days away."

The Seer said, "Go," and the man had no choice. He got on his tired horse and rode through the night.

Near morning he came to an inn. The man said, "I am tired. My horse is tired. We will stop for food and water and then we will rush on." In

the inn were nine other Jews. They begged the man to stay with them and be the tenth person in their minyan for Shabbat. He explained that the Seer had told him to go home, and he said, "Sorry, but no."

The man ate and drank, but fell asleep and woke just before Shabbat. He panicked when he realized that he was stuck. He became the tenth in their minyan.

It was an amazing Shabbat. When the group sang together it was as if angels were singing with them. When they danced together, it was as if they were dancing in the air. When they studied together, walls of fire surrounded them.

As soon as Shabbat was over, the man got back on his horse and rode through the night to get back to Lublin to apologize. When he got there the Seer was waiting. The Seer called him by name, and said, "You were supposed to die this Shabbat. That is why I wanted you to return home."

The man said, "I am still alive."

The Seer explained, "Sometimes a minyan has more power than a miracle-working rebbe."

From Martin Buber's *Tales of the Hasidim*

Questions

1. What do you think this story means?
2. Why is ten the right number for a minyan?
3. How does a minyan work miracles?
4. How can this story help you know where to point your heart when you say the בָּרְכוּ?

A Review

Some things to Know about the בָּרְכוּ

- All of the prayers before the בָּרְכוּ can be said by individuals. The בָּרְכוּ is the moment that the congregation forms a community to pray together.

- It takes a minyan, ten people, to say the בָּרְכוּ. It is a call and response, a dialogue between the prayer leader and the congregation.

- The בָּרְכוּ reminds us of the story of Ezra calling the Jewish people to finish rebuilding the Temple after the Babylonian Exile.

Language Learning

We learned or reviewed the following words:

before a direct object	and more		Adonai	
אֶת	וָעֶד	עוֹלָם	יי	בָּרוּךְ

We looked at the root  and the prefixes הַ and לְ .

We learned this prayer:

בָּרְכוּ אֶת־יי הַמְבֹרָךְ.

בָּרוּךְ יי הַמְבֹרָךְ לְעוֹלָם וָעֶד.

עֲצֹר!

42

Unit 4 — The שְׁמַע and Her בְּרָכוֹת

After the בָּרְכוּ, we enter a part of the service called the שְׁמַע **& Her** בְּרָכוֹת. This part of the service tells three big stories that are the themes of three prayers. These prayers are wrapped around a collection of Biblical texts, the שְׁמַע.

The first prayer is all about creation. It reminds us that we are living in a world that God created. When we say the יוֹצֵר אוֹר in the morning, we are like Adam and Eve looking out in amazement at the world around us. It is filled with miracles. Each and every thing we can see, hear, taste, smell, and touch contains a trace of God. By looking at creation we learn to understand the Creator. We too are God's creations. This first בְּרָכָה celebrates everything that God made and is still making.

The second בְּרָכָה is אַהֲבָה רַבָּה. It is about revelation. "Revelation" is a big word for communication. The prayer talks about the ways that God communicates wisdom to us. The big revelation moment was at Mt. Sinai when God gave the Torah to Israel. But there are many other Mt. Sinai moments in our lives. There are many other ways we come to understand things that God wants us to understand. Some of them we figure out on our own by studying and some of them we learn from other people. Sometimes, in some moments, we can almost hear God teaching us directly. This בְּרָכָה celebrates all of the Mt. Sinai moments in our lives.

In this unit you will learn the stories that surround the שְׁמַע.

43

The last בְּרָכָה, the גְּאֻלָּה, is about redemption. Redemption means "being rescued." Redemption is also a dream about a perfect world, one with peace and freedom, safety and plenty. We remember the time when God took us out of Egypt, and we believe that when people have finished working with God, there will be a final redemption. This last בְּרָכָה reminds us of the redemption from Egypt and directs us toward an even bigger redemption in the future. This בְּרָכָה is a celebration of all the times we have been freed from something that has enslaved us.

In the middle of this section is the שְׁמַע. The שְׁמַע begins with one sentence that says that God is One. The whole שְׁמַע is three paragraphs taken from all over the Torah. Each paragraph says that God gave us all of the מִצְוֹת. As a package, the blessings around the שְׁמַע tell us a history of the things that God has done: created the world, revealed the Torah, and liberated us from Egypt. When we put them together with the שְׁמַע, we remember that we bring these memories to life and build redemption in the future by doing the מִצְוֹת. The מִצְוֹת teach us about God, help us become good people, and guide us to work together to make a better world.

Questions

1. When was one time you noticed something that God made was amazing?
2. When was one time you felt like something major was revealed to you—that you suddenly understood something important?
3. When was one time that you felt you were rescued from a bad situation?
4. Why are these three ideas—creation, revelation, and redemption—important to talk about every day?

The Garden of Eden, Mt. Sinai, The Reed Sea

Rabbi Nahman of Bratzlav taught that the stories of creation, the giving of the Torah, and the escape from Egypt are not just things that happened long ago. They are also stories that happen in each of our own lives. We all have our own versions of being like Adam and Eve, learning Torah from God, and being set free. Here are some true stories.

Label the personal Creation story [C], the personal Mt. Sinai story [S], and the personal Exodus from Egypt story [E].

_____ My grandfather was in the Russian Army. Most Jews who were drafted into the Russian Army disappeared. They never came back home. That is why rich Jews paid bribes so that their sons would not have to go into the Army. My grandfather went and came back. He said that the secret was "mandelbread." His mother sent him a package of his favorite baked goods, her mandelbread. Someone stole it. He got so angry that he made a plan and just escaped.

_____ When I was a little girl I would have a Shabbat dinner and then go to synagogue. My reward was that I would fall asleep on my father's shoulder. He would carry me out and when I woke up we would dance. Then dad would carry me upstairs. I would smell of sweat and cologne and love. That has always been my ultimate Shabbat experience.

_____ My dad owned a bar. To keep his liquor license he had to pay off the party bosses and help them buy votes. When it was time for me to go to college he asked a Senator for help getting me into university around the Jewish quotas they used to have. The Senator showed him a list and asked him to pick the person who was to be knocked off so that I could have a place. My dad said, "No," and started to walk out. The Senator stopped him and gave me a place. That moment is one of the most important things my father ever taught me.

45

A סִדוּר Treasure Hunt

Using a copy of the סִדוּר used in your congregation for שַׁבָּת morning, find the page numbers of the following prayers. These are the prayers we are going to study this year.

מוֹדֶה אֲנִי _____

מַה טֹּבוּ _____

בָּרְכוּ _____

יוֹצֵר אוֹר _____

אַהֲבָה רַבָּה _____

שְׁמַע _____

וְאָהַבְתָּ _____

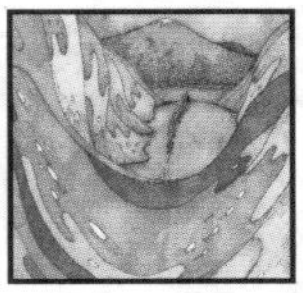

מִי־כָמֹכָה _____

עֲצֹר!

יוֹצֵר אוֹר

יוֹצֵר אוֹר is:

- the first of two בְּרָכוֹת before the שְׁמַע in the morning,
- a בְּרָכָה about the creation of light,
- a memory of the Garden of Eden,
- a look at good and evil in the world,
- a glance at a better future.

The traditional יוֹצֵר אוֹר is a long prayer that gets even longer on Shabbat. In the Reform siddur (and in some other prayerbooks), a shorter version is used. We will only look at part of the prayer in this book.

יוֹצֵר אוֹר is about light. Light means many things. Light was the first thing that God created. Everything started with light. When we thank God for making the light, we are also thanking God for all of creation.

When we speak of light and darkness, we are also talking about good and evil. Darkness stands for evil, the place where God seems to be missing. Light is the place where people are connected to God and do what is right.

Light also stands for learning and wisdom. When people gain knowledge, we call them "enlightened." For Jews, the Torah is the central wisdom that God wants us to have. We also say and sing תּוֹרָה אוֹרָה, the "Torah is light".

A midrash that you will read later in this chapter tells us that Adam and Eve were the first ones to say the יוֹצֵר אוֹר. The first יוֹצֵר אוֹר was in the Garden of Eden. It spoke of creation and good and evil.

In this unit you will learn
- about יוֹצֵר אוֹר
- two roots
- one story about creation.

יוֹצֵר אוֹר is a very long prayer. Here are a few parts of the text to practice.

BLESSED are You, ADONAI, our God, RULER of the COSMOS	בָּרוּךְ אַתָּה יי אֱלֹהֵינוּ מֶלֶךְ הָעוֹלָם .1
The One-Who-Radiates LIGHT and creates DARKNESS	יוֹצֵר אוֹר וּבוֹרֵא חֹשֶׁךְ .2
The One-Who-Makes PEACE and Who creates EVERYTHING.	עֹשֶׂה שָׁלוֹם וּבוֹרֵא אֶת הַכֹּל. .3
The One-Who-LIGHTS the earth	הַמֵּאִיר לָאָרֶץ .4
and her residents in mercy,	וְלַדָּרִים עָלֶיהָ בְּרַחֲמִים .5
in GOODNESS (God) makes ANEW	וּבְטוּבוֹ מְחַדֵּשׁ .6
every single day—always—the makings of CREATION.	בְּכָל יוֹם תָּמִיד מַעֲשֵׂה בְרֵאשִׁית. .7
Your makings are great, ADONAI	מַה רַבּוּ מַעֲשֶׂיךָ יי .8
You made all of them WISELY	כֻּלָּם בְּחָכְמָה עָשִׂיתָ .9
the earth is filled with Your possessions.	מָלְאָה הָאָרֶץ קִנְיָנֶךָ. .10
Be BLESSED, ADONAI, our God	תִּתְבָּרַךְ יי אֱלֹהֵינוּ .11
for the glory of the makings of Your hands	עַל שֶׁבַח מַעֲשֵׂה יָדֶיךָ .12
and for the brightness of the LIGHTS which You made	וְעַל מְאוֹרֵי אוֹר שֶׁעָשִׂיתָ .13
May they exalt You—So be it!	יְפָאֲרוּךָ סֶּלָה. .14
BLESSED are You, ADONAI, The ONE-Who-Radiates LIGHTS.	בָּרוּךְ אַתָּה יי יוֹצֵר הַמְּאוֹרוֹת .15

יוֹצֵר אוֹר: The opening of this prayer comes from a lesson that the prophet Isaiah taught. Isaiah said that God says, "I am the Eternal and there is no One else. (1) I radiate light and create darkness. (2) I make peace and create evil." Isaiah thought that it was important to teach that God created "evil" as well as good. How can a good God be the source of all the evil in the world?

Later, when the prayerbook was assembled, the rabbis changed the words "created evil" to "creates all (including evil)." Their big concern was a Persian religion that believed in two gods, a good god and an evil god. People were reading the two sentences in this prayer as if each applied to a different god. By changing "evil" to "all" there is no doubt that God created everything. What was gained by this change? What was lost?

מְחַדֵּשׁ בְּכָל-יוֹם תָּמִיד. The **יוֹצֵר** says that creation continues every single day. God did not create the world and then walk away. God is always creating. How do you understand that idea? How can you see it as a true statement?

48

בְּרָא is one of the first roots in the Torah. God does it all the time.

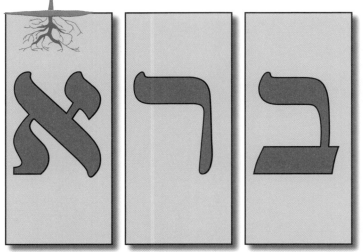

Can you see the three letters בְּרָא in these words?

בְּרִיאָה   לִבְרֹא   בּוֹרֵא

Hebrew builds words out of three-letter roots.

בּוֹרֵא = create

לִבְרֹא = to create

בְּרִיאָה = a creation

Find and circle the words with the root בְּרָא.

1. הַמְבֹרָךְ   מַלְכוּתוֹ   בּוֹרְאֶךָ   כָּבוֹד   בָּרוּךְ   בּוֹרֵא

2. הַבְּרִיאוֹת   עַל   לִבְרֹא   הָאָרֶץ   לְהַדְלִיק   אֱלֹהִים

3. חֹשֶׁךְ   וּבוֹרֵא   אוֹר   יוֹצֵר   בַּר   בָּרָא   הַגָּפֶן   פְּרִי

4. מִצְוָה   בָּרְכוּ   בְּרִיאָה   הַשָּׁמַיִם   בְּרֵאשִׁית   כְּמַלְכֵּנוּ

Now recite these בְּרָא phrases from the Torah.

5. בְּרֵאשִׁית בָּרָא אֱלֹהִים אֵת הַשָּׁמַיִם וְאֵת הָאָרֶץ.

6. וַיִּבְרָא אֱלֹהִים אֶת־הַתַּנִּינִם הַגְּדֹלִים וְאֵת כָּל־נֶפֶשׁ הַחַיָּה הָרֹמֶשֶׂת

7. וַיִּבְרָא אֱלֹהִים אֶת־הָאָדָם בְּצַלְמוֹ בְּצֶלֶם אֱלֹהִים בָּרָא אֹתוֹ

49

בָּרוּךְ

אַתָּה

מֶלֶךְ

עוֹלָם

אוֹר

חֹשֶׁךְ

עֲצֹר!

Here is the first line of the יוֹצֵר אוֹר. Use the vocabulary to create your own translation.

Take your best guess at these meanings. Your teacher will help you fill in the parts you don't yet know.

בָּרוּךְ אַתָּה יי אֱלֹהֵינוּ מֶלֶךְ הָעוֹלָם

יוֹצֵר אוֹר וּבוֹרֵא חֹשֶׁךְ

עֹשֶׂה שָׁלוֹם וּבוֹרֵא אֶת-הַכֹּל.

My best guess at the meaning of this prayer is:

_____

_____

_____

To Talk About

1. The יוֹצֵר אוֹר is a sunrise prayer. Think back to a great sunrise experience you have had. What is your sunrise memory? How can this memory help you to point your heart when you say the יוֹצֵר אוֹר?

2. There are two words for creating things. בּוֹרֵא is an act of creation that only God can perform. יוֹצֵר is an act of creation that both God and people can accomplish. List some יוֹצֵר things and some בּוֹרֵא things. Why do you think this prayer begins with יוֹצֵר?

(word parts)	(words)	(verbs)
the = הַ/הָ	Adonai = יי	creates = בּוֹרֵא
and = וְ/וּ	our God = אֱלֹהֵינוּ	בּוֹרֵא is only for God
If you have time, go back to page 48 and practice the complete יוֹצֵר אוֹר.	do or make = עוֹשֶׂה	creates = יוֹצֵר
	Peace = שָׁלוֹם	יוֹצֵר can be done by either people or God
	all = כָּל/כֹּל	

Go back to page 48 and read the יוֹצֵר אוֹר before you work on this story.

Adam and Eve's First Shabbat

Adam and Eve were created about two hours before sundown before the first Shabbat. In one hour, they managed to fall in love, eat the fruit from the one tree they had been told to avoid, and make God really angry.

Just before Shabbat was ready to begin, God was prepared to kick them out of the Garden. Adam and Eve were really scared. When they were created, the sun was yellow and high in the sky. Now it was blood red and sinking toward the horizon. They were terrified because they believed God was punishing them. They thought God was uncreating the world, and they would be in darkness forever.

Just as God got ready to kick them out of the Garden, Shabbat stepped in. She said, "You promised me that I would not be alone. Everyone else has a partner. Sunday has Monday. Tuesday has Wednesday. Thursday has Friday. Only I am alone. You promised me that Israel would be with me. If you kick Adam and Eve out of the Garden before they experience this Shabbat, Israel will never know how wonderful I can be. I will be too much effort, because they will not know my reward."

God agreed. "Adam and Eve can spend this Shabbat in the Garden, then they will have to leave."

As the sun set, God showed Adam and Eve how to light Shabbat candles. This was the first fire. They then walked together around the garden and God showed off all the things that had been created. God even introduced them to Shoshana, the macaw. Together they sat down and ate Shabbat dinner. God told Adam and Eve that everything would be fine. God tucked them in to go to sleep. The midrash even tells us that "God braided Eve's hair."

The two of them heard God's words, "Things will be okay," but they did not believe them. They did not sleep at all. They tossed and turned all night. It was the longest night—I'll bet you know that kind of night. They thought and thought about what they had done and they felt really bad about the way they had acted.

The night seemed to last forever. Then suddenly there was gray at the edges of the black. Then the night was edged in blue. They could see things again. At last the edge of the sun sparked between two mountains, and Adam and Eve realized that the world had not been destroyed. As they faced the new day, their new chance, they said together, "Praised are You...the One-Who Radiates light and creates darkness, the One-Who Makes peace and even creates evil."

Later, God would teach Isaiah those same words. Even later, the rabbis who arranged the siddur would use them as the prayer to greet the morning light, because they knew that in some way, every morning is like that first Shabbat morning that greeted Adam and Eve. It is a chance to start over.

From the Midrash, with a touch of Danny Siegel

Questions

1. What do you think that first Shabbat morning meant to Adam and Eve?
2. When have you felt that way?
3. How can remembering this story help you find a way to point your heart when you say this prayer?

Beginnings

This is the first sentence of the Torah. Draw your own picture of its meaning.

בְּרֵאשִׁית
בָּרָא
אֱלֹהִים
אֵת הַשָּׁמַיִם
וְאֵת הָאָרֶץ.

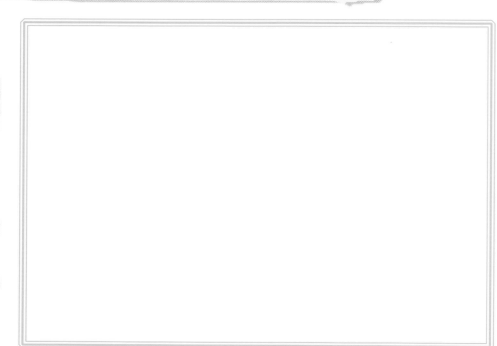

Sunrise

יוֹצֵר אוֹר is a prayer about sunrise.
Write yur own sunrise story.

_____

_____

_____

_____

_____

_____

_____

_____

_____

עֲצֹר!

53

אוֹר is another important root.

Can you see the three letters אוֹר in these words?

הַמֵּאִיר   מְאוֹרֵי   מְאוֹרוֹת

Sometimes the וֹ drops out.

Hebrew builds words out of three-letter roots.

the One-Who lights = הַמֵּאִיר

from the lights of = מְאוֹרֵי

lights = מְאוֹרוֹת

Circle the words with the root אוֹר.

1. אוֹר   יוֹצֵר   בּוֹרֵא   עוֹשֶׂה   מְאוֹרוֹת   הֵאִיר   הַבְּרִיאוֹת

2. עַל   מְאוֹרֵי   הָאֵשׁ   יָאוֹר   לָאָרֶץ   שָׁלוֹם   הָאָר   אוֹצָר

3. אַהֲבָה   רַבָּה   וְהָאֵר   עֵינֵינוּ   הַמְּאוֹרוֹת   הַמֵּאִיר   בִּירְאָה

4. הוּאָר   תָּמִיד   עוֹלָם   תָּאִיר   לְאוֹרוֹ   תּוֹרָה   אוֹרָה

Hidden Light

The Torah tells us that God created light on the first day. It also tells us that God created the sun, moon, and stars on the fourth day. For the first three days the world had a very strange kind of light—light that came directly from God.

The Talmud tells us that when one looked at things in this light, one could see from one side of forever to the other side of forever. When people started to do evil things, God hid this light away so that it would not be used in the wrong way. We are told that in the future, righteous people will again get to use this light.

The Baal Shem Tov said that God hid this light in the Torah. How can light be hidden in the Torah? How can Torah help you see from one side of forever to the other?

(EIN YAAKOV, HAGGIGAH)

54

Go back to page 48 and practice the יוֹצֵר אוֹר before you work on this page.

Recite these phrases with אוֹר in them.

1. אוֹר חָדָשׁ עַל צִיּוֹן תָּאִיר ‏ ‏ יוֹצֵר אוֹר וּבוֹרֵא חֹשֶׁךְ

2. וְהָאֵר עֵינֵינוּ בְּתוֹרָתֶךָ ‏ ‏ וְנִזְכֶּה כֻלָּנוּ מְהֵרָה לְאוֹרוֹ

3. אוֹר זָרֻעַ לַצַּדִּיק וּלְיִשְׁרֵי לֵב שִׂמְחָה ‏ ‏ הַמֵּאִיר לָאָרֶץ וְלַדָּרִים עָלֶיהָ

4. קָרָא לַשֶּׁמֶשׁ וַיִּזְרַח אוֹר ‏ ‏ טוֹבִים מְאוֹרוֹת שֶׁבָּרָא אֱלֹהֵינוּ

5. בּוֹרֵא יוֹם וָלַיְלָה גּוֹלֵל אוֹר מִפְּנֵי חֹשֶׁךְ וְחֹשֶׁךְ מִפְּנֵי אוֹר

6. בָּרוּךְ אַתָּה יי אֱלֹהֵינוּ מֶלֶךְ הָעוֹלָם בּוֹרֵא מְאוֹרֵי הָאֵשׁ

Write in the missing letters for these words built from the root אוֹר.

8. הַמְּ__וֹרוֹת ‏ ‏ 7. א__רָה

10. הָ__ֵר ‏ ‏ 9. הַמֵּאִי__

12. מְאוֹ__ֵ__י ‏ ‏ 11. א__ר

The Answer to Hidden Light

The Baal Shem Tov taught that if you point your heart in the right direction, you can find the hidden light when you study Torah. This means that finding God's light is not just about knowing things but also about taking them into your soul.

When you study Torah and really understand its teaching, you can see all the way from creation to the end of history. The end of history is when people finally live together in peace and cooperation, with more than enough of everything for everyone.

A Review

Some things to Know about יוֹצֵר אוֹר

- It is the first בְּרָכָה after the בָּרְכוּ in a morning service. It is also the first of two בְּרָכוֹת that come before the שְׁמַע.

- It is a בְּרָכָה about creation, a בְּרָכָה connected to sunrise.

- יוֹצֵר אוֹר is also a בְּרָכָה about light. Light means more than just physical light. It is also a way of talking about knowledge and thinking about good and evil. יוֹצֵר אוֹר includes both of these meanings.

Language Learning

Some of the words we learned or reviewed in this lesson are:

חֹשֶׁךְ   אוֹר   עוֹלָם   מֶלֶךְ   אַתָּה   בָּרוּךְ

We looked at the roots  בּרא , אוֹר  and the prefixes הַ , הָ and וּ .

Prayer Meaning

We looked at the meaning of the first sentence of יוֹצֵר אוֹר and talked about its connection to Adam and Eve and to Isaiah.

בָּרוּךְ אַתָּה יי אֱלֹהֵינוּ מֶלֶךְ הָעוֹלָם יוֹצֵר אוֹר וּבוֹרֵא חֹשֶׁךְ

עוֹשֶׂה שָׁלוֹם וּבוֹרֵא אֶת הַכֹּל.

The opening sentence comes from Isaiah with the change of the word רָע for הַכֹּל. The Midrash teaches that Adam and Eve were the first ones to speak these words.

עֲצֹר!

56

אַהֲבָה רַבָּה

אַהֲבָה רַבָּה is:
- the second of two morning בְּרָכוֹת before the שְׁמַע,
- a בְּרָכָה about God's love for Israel,
- a memory of Mount Sinai,
- a statement about the power of studying Torah,
- a look at the relationship that Torah creates between God and Israel.

It was at Mount Sinai that God gave us the gift of Torah. Torah shows us that God loves us—because in it God gave us the wisdom we need to live a good life.

Torah makes us God's partner. When the Jews received the Torah, they agreed to work with God to make the world into the best possible place. Torah is a book of directions on how to change ourselves into the best people we can be and on how to change the world into the best place we all can make it. Torah creates a contract. When we accepted the Torah we agreed to work with God to create a world of peace, justice, freedom, and prosperity.

Mount Sinai was the moment that Israel first knew that God loved them. That love came in a book, the Torah.

אַהֲבָה רַבָּה talks about our relationship with God. It reminds us that through the Torah we can be close to God.

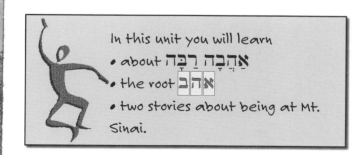

In this unit you will learn
- about אַהֲבָה רַבָּה
- the root אהב
- two stories about being at Mt. Sinai.

57

אַהֲבָה רַבָּה

1.	אַהֲבָה רַבָּה אֲהַבְתָּנוּ, יְיָ אֱלֹהֵינוּ,
With much LOVE You have LOVED us, ADONAI, our God,	
2.	חֶמְלָה גְדוֹלָה וִיתֵרָה
With great COMPASSION and more	
3.	חָמַלְתָּ עָלֵינוּ. אָבִינוּ מַלְכֵּנוּ,
You have had COMPASSION on us. Our PARENT, our Ruler,	
4.	בַּעֲבוּר אֲבוֹתֵינוּ שֶׁבָּטְחוּ בְךָ
for the sake of our PARENTS who trusted in You—	
5.	וַתְּלַמְּדֵם חֻקֵּי חַיִּים
and whom You taught the rules of life—	
6.	כֵּן תְּחָנֵּנוּ וּתְלַמְּדֵנוּ.
also (A) be gracious to us and TEACH us.	
7.	אָבִינוּ, הָאָב הָרַחֲמָן
Our PARENT, the MERCIFUL PARENT,	
8.	הַמְרַחֵם, רַחֵם עָלֵינוּ
The ONE-Who-is-MERCIFUL (B) have MERCY on us.	
9.	וְתֵן בְּלִבֵּנוּ
(Please) (C) give (in) our hearts	
10.	לְהָבִין וּלְהַשְׂכִּיל, לִשְׁמוֹעַ
(1) to understand, (2) to reason, (3) to hear,	
11.	לִלְמֹד וּלְלַמֵּד לִשְׁמֹר
(4) to be TAUGHT, (5) to TEACH, (6) to keep,	
12.	וְלַעֲשׂוֹת, וּלְקַיֵּם
(7) to do, (8) to make permanent	
13.	אֶת כָּל דִּבְרֵי תַלְמוּד תּוֹרָתֶךָ בְּאַהֲבָה.
all the words of the TEACHING of Your Torah, in LOVE.	
14.	וְהָאֵר עֵינֵינוּ בְּתוֹרָתֶךָ
(D) Enlighten our eyes with Your Torah	
15.	וְדַבֵּק לִבֵּנוּ בְּמִצְוֹתֶיךָ
and (E) make Your mitzvot stick to our hearts	
16.	וְיַחֵד לְבָבֵנוּ לְאַהֲבָה
and (F) unify our hearts to LOVE	
17.	וּלְיִרְאָה אֶת שְׁמֶךָ.
and to be in AWE of Your NAME.	

And (please) (G) don't let us be embarrassed, ever—	וְלֹא נֵבוֹשׁ לְעוֹלָם וָעֶד	18.
because in Your holy NAME,	כִּי בְשֵׁם קָדְשְׁךָ	19.
which is GREAT and AWESOME, we trust.	הַגָּדוֹל וְהַנּוֹרָא בָּטָחְנוּ	20.
We will REJOICE AND BE HAPPY IN YOUR SALVATION.	נָגִילָה וְנִשְׂמְחָה בִּישׁוּעָתֶךָ.	21.
(H) And (please) bring us in peace	וַהֲבִיאֵנוּ לְשָׁלוֹם	22.
from the four corners of the earth	מֵאַרְבַּע כַּנְפוֹת הָאָרֶץ,	23.
and make us go and establish our land—	וְתוֹלִיכֵנוּ קוֹמְמִיּוּת לְאַרְצֵנוּ.	24.
because You are God, The ONE-Who-Works at SALVATION,	כִּי אֵל פּוֹעֵל יְשׁוּעוֹת אָתָּה,	25.
and You have CHOSEN us from all peoples	וּבָנוּ בָחַרְתָּ מִכָּל עַם	26.
and language groupings,	וְלָשׁוֹן	27.
and You have brought us close to Your GREAT NAME	וְקֵרַבְתָּנוּ לְשִׁמְךָ הַגָּדוֹל	28.
in truth, so be it—	סֶלָה בֶּאֱמֶת,	29.
to give thanks to You and to Your ONENESS in LOVE.	לְהוֹדוֹת לְךָ וּלְיַחֶדְךָ בְּאַהֲבָה.	30.
BLESSED are You, ADONAI,	בָּרוּךְ אַתָּה יי	31.
The ONE-Who-CHOOSES the People Israel, in LOVE.	הַבּוֹחֵר בְּעַמּוֹ יִשְׂרָאֵל בְּאַהֲבָה.	32.

A medieval Jewish philosopher, Saadia Gaon taught, "יוֹצֵר אוֹר speaks of God in the third person. In אַהֲבָה רַבָּה the point-of-view changes. We now call God 'You.'" אַהֲבָה רַבָּה speaks of God choosing Israel and Israel choosing God in love. It is very much like a wedding. It is as if we are saying, "I _____ (fill in your name) take You, Adonai, to be my Deity—to love and to cherish, to honor and obey." How is our relationship to God like a marriage?

Yehudah ha-Levi, another medieval Jewish philosopher, taught that our job is to think of God's love as light, and that each Jew needs to think of himself or herself as a mirror. Can you explain Yehudah ha-Levi's interpretation in your own words?

The root אהב is at the heart of this בְּרָכָה.

Can you see the three letters אהב in these words?

וְאָהַבְתָ   אֲהַבְתָנוּ   אַהֲבָה

Hebrew builds words out of three-letter roots.

love = אַהֲבָה

You have loved us = אֲהַבְתָנוּ

and you shall love = וְאָהַבְתָ

Look at these words and circle all that contain the root אהב.

1. וְאָהַבְתָ   קְדֻשָׁה   יוֹצֵר   בָּרָא   קָדוֹשׁ   אוֹהֵב

2. אַהֲבַת   מַלְכוּתְךָ   אַהֲבָה   אֱלֹהֵינוּ   הִתְאַהֵב   בִּרְכַּת

3. אָהוּב   אָהוֹב   אֲהַבְתָנוּ   מֶלֶךְ   גֶפֶן   אֲהָבִים

Recite these אהב phrases.

4. וְיַחֵד לְבָבֵנוּ לְאַהֲבָה וּלְיִרְאָה אֶת שְׁמֶךָ

5. אַהֲבַת עוֹלָם בֵּית יִשְׂרָאֵל עַמְּךָ אָהָבְתָ

6. אַהֲבָה רַבָּה אֲהַבְתָנוּ יי אֱלֹהֵינוּ חֶמְלָה גְדוֹלָה וִיתֵרָה

7. וְאָהַבְתָ אֵת יי אֱלֹהֶיךָ בְּכָל-לְבָבְךָ וּבְכָל-נַפְשְׁךָ וּבְכָל-מְאֹדֶךָ

עֲצֹר!

60

Go back to pages 58-59 and practice the אַהֲבָה רַבָּה before you work on this page.

Word Endings

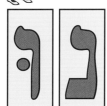

Look at the two letters נוּ
at the end of these
two words:

לִבֵּנוּ   עֵינֵינוּ
our hearts   our eyes

נוּ means "our" or "us."

Look at the letter ךָ
at the end of these
two words:

בְּתוֹרָתֶךָ   שְׁמֶךָ
Your name   Your Torah

ךָ means "your."

Circle the words that end with נוּ and underline those with ךָ.

1. וְהָאֵר עֵינֵינוּ בְּתוֹרָתֶךָ לְבָבֵנוּ אֵת אֲבוֹתֵינוּ וְדַבֵּק

2. אֱלֹהֵנוּ וּלְיִרְאָה לִבֵּנוּ שְׁמֶךָ לְאַהֲבָה אֱלֹהֶיךָ בְּמִצְוֹתֶיךָ

What word means "Your Torah"? _____ .

What word means our "hearts"?_____ .

Incognito Words and Root Words

Some Hebrew words and root words change a little. ה, ו and י can drop out of the word.
Circle the word on each line that is built from the word in the colored box.

3.	**1** אֶחָד	(וְיַחֵד)	לִבָבֵנוּ	אֵת	וְדַבֵּק	לִבֵּנוּ	בְּתוֹרָתֶךָ
4.	**לֵב**	וְהָאֵר	עֵינֵינוּ	וּלְיִרְאָה	אֵת	לִבֵּנוּ	שְׁמֶךָ
5.	**אוֹר**	לְאַהֲבָה	בְּתוֹרָתֶךָ	וְהָאֵר	לִבָבֵנוּ	וְדַבֵּק
6.	command **צוה**	לִבָבֵנוּ	וְהָאֵר	וְדַבֵּק	לְאַהֲבָה	בְּמִצְוֹתֶיךָ
7.	**עֵינַיִם**	שְׁמֶךָ	וּלְיִרְאָה	עֵינֵינוּ	לִבֵּנוּ	לְאַהֲבָה

61

אוֹר

עֵינַיִם

תּוֹרָה

דַּבֵּק

לֵב

1

אֶחָד

אָהַב

Take your best guess at the meaning of this text. Your teacher will help you with your translation.

וְהָאֵר עֵינֵינוּ בְּתוֹרָתֶךָ
וְדַבֵּק לִבֵּנוּ בְּמִצְוֹתֶיךָ
וְיַחֵד לְבָבֵנוּ לְאַהֲבָה
וּלְיִרְאָה אֶת שְׁמֶךָ.

My best guess at the meaning of this prayer is:

_____

_____

_____

_____

To Talk About

The prayer asks something that seems strange. It asks God to help us make our heart אֶחָד. We want that oneness to include both יִרְאָה and אַהֲבָה of God.

Is it possible to have both אַהֲבָה and יִרְאָה at the same time? Why do we want both of those feelings about God?

(word parts)

and = וְ/וּ
us/our = נוּ
to = לְ

your = ךָ
in/with = בְּ

(words)

awe = יִרְאָה
name = שֵׁם
mitzvot = מִצְוֹת

Two Memories of Sinai

Sometimes different people remember the same event differently. The Jewish people have two different memories of receiving the Torah at Mt. Sinai.

Here is the first memory: The Torah is very demanding. It asks people to do many things that are not easy, and it asks people not to do many things that are not easy to stop yourself from doing.

God went to a lot of different people and asked them to accept the Torah. Each group asked about the Torah, and God repeated one or two of its rules. Each time God described the Torah, the people who heard about it politely said, "No, thank you!" There were things the Torah asked them to do that they did not want to do. There were things the Torah asked them do that they did not want to stop doing. Israel was God's last chance. Everyone else had said, "No, thank you!"

The Families-of-Israel were at Mt. Sinai. They said, "No, thank you." This time God was prepared. God lifted up the mountain and held it over their heads. It hung in the air like a huge, open coffin. God said to Israel, "Do you want to accept my Torah, or do you want me to put the mountain down?"

It was at that moment, with Mt. Sinai hanging over their heads, that the Families-of-Israel said, "We will do it and we will obey it." That is how Israel accepted the Torah.

The second memory is very different. Israel really wanted the Torah. They believed that it would be fun to celebrate all the holidays. They thought that it would be an honor to become God's partner. Just like little kids, Israel jumped up and down and hollered, "Choose me! Pick me!"

God said to Israel, "Why should I pick you? The Torah is really valuable. Who will promise that you will treat it well? Who will guarantee that you will not ruin it?"

Israel said, "Abraham, Sarah, Isaac, Rebekkah, Leah, Rachel, and Jacob will be responsible."

God answered, "Every one of them broke the rules of the Torah at some point and did something wrong. They are not the ones to protect My Torah."

Israel said, "How about the prophets? They all taught Your word."

God answered, "They told you the right things to do, and you usually did not listen to them. If you won't listen to the prophets, how can I make them responsible?"

Finally, Israel had a big conference and said to God, "Our children will be the ones to take responsibility. They promise that they will study the Torah and take it into their hearts. They promise to make the future better."

God thought about it and then said, "The Torah is yours."

As God gave them the Torah, the Families-of-Israel shouted out, "We will do it and we will obey it." That is how Israel accepted the Torah.

From the Midrash

Questions

1. Have you ever felt like you were trapped in the first memory of Mt. Sinai—as if being Jewish is something you are forced to do?
2. Have you ever felt like you were living the second memory, proud and privileged to be Jewish?
3. Why do we need both stories? How can both memories help us to say the אַהֲבָה רַבָּה?

עֲצֹר!

Go back to pages 58-59 and practice the אַהֲבָה רַבָּה before you work on this page.

A נוּ Adventure

1. תַּלְמְדֵנוּ אֲבוֹתֵינוּ אָבִינוּ מַלְכֵּנוּ עָלֵינוּ אֲהַבְתָּנוּ אֱלֹהֵינוּ

2. וְתוֹלִיכֵנוּ וַהֲבִיאֵנוּ בְּטַחְנוּ לְבָבֵנוּ לִבֵּנוּ עֵינֵינוּ בְּלִבֵּנוּ

3. נִשְׁמוֹתֵינוּ כְּמוֹשִׁיעֵנוּ אֲנַחְנוּ כְּמַלְכֵּנוּ וְקָרַבְתָּנוּ וּבָנוּ

4. אַהֲבָה רַבָּה אֲהַבְתָּנוּ יְיָ אֱלֹהֵינוּ חֶמְלָה גְדוֹלָה וִיתֵרָה חָמַלְתָּ עָלֵינוּ

5. וְתֵן בְּלִבֵּנוּ לְהָבִין וּלְהַשְׂכִּיל וְהָאֵר עֵינֵינוּ בְּתוֹרָתֶךָ

6. וְדַבֵּק לִבֵּנוּ בְּמִצְוֹתֶיךָ וַהֲבִיאֵנוּ לְשָׁלוֹם מֵאַרְבַּע כַּנְפוֹת

7. וְתוֹלִיכֵנוּ קוֹמְמִיּוּת לְאַרְצֵנוּ וּבָנוּ בָחַרְתָּ מִכָּל עַם וְלָשׁוֹן

8. אִלּוּ הוֹצִיאָנוּ מִמִּצְרַיִם דַּיֵּנוּ אִלּוּ נָתַן לָנוּ אֶת הַשַּׁבָּת דַּיֵּנוּ

9. אִלּוּ נָתַן לָנוּ אֶת הַתּוֹרָה דַּיֵּנוּ אִלּוּ הִכְנִיסָנוּ לְאֶרֶץ יִשְׂרָאֵל דַּיֵּנוּ

Which word means:

our God _____   our eyes _____

in Your Torah _____   in Your mitzvot _____

our Ruler _____   in our hearts _____

Why do you think אַהֲבָה רַבָּה is filled with words that end with נוּ?

Reading from the Torah

Here are some prayer phrases that come from the Torah. Practice the phrases with and without the vowels.

1. שְׁמַע יִשְׂרָאֵל יי אֱלֹהֵינוּ יי אֶחָד

2. **שמע ישראל יי אלהינו יי אחד**

3. וְאָהַבְתָּ אֵת יי אֱלֹהֶיךָ
בְּכָל־לְבָבְךָ וּבְכָל־נַפְשְׁךָ וּבְכָל־מְאֹדֶךָ

4. **ואהבת את יי אלהיך
בכל לבבך ובכל נפשך ובכל מאדך**

5. מִי כָמֹכָה בָּאֵלִם יי מִי כָּמֹכָה נֶאְדָּר בַּקֹּדֶשׁ

6. **מי כמכה באלם יי מי כמכה נאדר בקדש**

7. מַה טֹּבוּ אֹהָלֶיךָ יַעֲקֹב מִשְׁכְּנֹתֶיךָ יִשְׂרָאֵל

8. **מה טבו אהליך יעקב משכנתיך ישראל**

Mt. Sinai Moments

A rabbi named Yehudah Aryeh Leib Alter, who was called the *S'fat Emet*, taught, "Every person has his or her own piece of Torah." He explained, "The complete Torah was given to the Jewish people as a whole. However, each person has a personal teaching, his or her own Torah, inside them. This is hidden within the soul. There is a piece of Torah that can be learned from every person."

How can God's word be hidden in each and every person?

My Mt. Sinai Moment

A Mt. Sinai moment is a time when you suddenly learn a great truth. It is when you understand one of the things that God wants you to understand. Sometimes another person teaches you this lesson. Sometimes you learn from something that happens. Sometimes you just know. Describe one of your own Mt. Sinai moments.

_____

_____

_____

_____

_____

A Review

Some Things to Know about אַהֲבָה רַבָּה

- It is the second of two בְּרָכוֹת that are said before the שְׁמַע in a morning service.
- It is a memory of being at Mt. Sinai and receiving the gift of the Torah.
- אַהֲבָה רַבָּה teaches that giving of rules can show love.

Language Learning

Some of the words we learned or reviewed in this lesson are:

יִרְאָה awe   אֶחָד 1   לֵב   דְבֵּק   תּוֹרָה   עֵינַיִם   אוֹר   אַהֲבָה

מִצְוֹת mitzvot   שֵׁם name

We looked at the following root אהב ,

and the prefixes וְ, לְ, בְּ ; and the suffixes נוּ and ךָ .

Prayer Meaning

We looked at one part of אַהֲבָה רַבָּה . It is these words that we often sing aloud.

וְהָאֵר עֵינֵינוּ בְּתוֹרָתֶךָ וְדַבֵּק לִבֵּנוּ בְּמִצְוֹתֶיךָ וְיַחֵד לְבָבֵנוּ
לְאַהֲבָה וּלְיִרְאָה אֶת שְׁמֶךָ.

When we studied יוֹצֵר אוֹר we learned about the light of creation. This part of the prayer teaches us that Torah is another kind of light.

עֲצֹר!

68

שְׁמַע

The **שְׁמַע** is probably the most important sentence in the whole Torah. It states the single most important Jewish idea—there is only One God.

The **שְׁמַע** is also a collection of three paragraphs in the Torah that come from three different places and were brought together to be the heart of one part of the morning and evening services. The three-paragraph **שְׁמַע** was created to solve a problem.

Originally, back in the time of the Temple, the Ten Commandments were recited as part of the Temple service every day. It was a big performance remembering being at Mt. Sinai. People began to take the Ten Commandments too seriously. They began to believe that they were the only important **מִצְוֹת**. They would say, "I am a good Jew, I do the big ten," and not bother with the rest of the 613 **מִצְוֹת**. The rabbis of the Talmud knew that they had to make a change.

They found three passages in the Torah that all said **כָּל מִצְוֹתַי**, "all My commandments." They replaced the Ten Commandments with this new collection of passages.

The **שְׁמַע** teaches us that God is One. It then makes sure that we live that Oneness at every moment of the day, everywhere we go, with everyone we meet, through everything we do.

How can you live the truth that God is One?

In this unit you will learn
• about the שְׁמַע
• the root שׁמע
• a story about the שְׁמַע

69

Can you see the three letters שְׁמַע in these words?

שׁוֹמֵעַ   שְׁמַע   לִשְׁמֹעַ

Hebrew builds words out of three-letter roots.

to listen = לִשְׁמֹעַ

listen! (command) = שְׁמַע

listens = שׁוֹמֵעַ

Practice these words and circle all that contain the root שְׁמַע.

1. אֶחָד   לִשְׁמֹעַ   כָּבוֹד   בָּרְכוּ   הִשְׁתַּמֵּעַ   מַלְכֵי

2. נִשְׁמַע   וָעֶד   כְּמוֹשִׁיעֵנוּ   הַמְבֹרָךְ   מַלְכֵּנוּ   יִשְׁמְעוּ

3. כְּמַלְכֵּנוּ   שׁוֹמֵעַ   אֵין   שְׁמַע   קוֹלֵנוּ   מַה   נִשְׁמַע

Practice these parts of the שְׁמַע.

4. שְׁמַע יִשְׂרָאֵל   מַלְכוּתוֹ   יי אֶחָד   שֵׁם כָּבוֹד

5. בָּרוּךְ שֵׁם כָּבוֹד   לְעוֹלָם וָעֶד   יי אֱלֹהֵינוּ   שְׁמַע יִשְׂרָאֵל

6. שְׁמַע יִשְׂרָאֵל יי אֱלֹהֵינוּ יי אֶחָד

7. בָּרוּךְ שֵׁם כְּבוֹד מַלְכוּתוֹ לְעוֹלָם וָעֶד

Your teacher will help you with your translation.

שְׁמַע יִשְׂרָאֵל יי אֱלֹהֵינוּ יי אֶחָד.
בָּרוּךְ שֵׁם כְּבוֹד מַלְכוּתוֹ לְעוֹלָם וָעֶד.

My best guess at the meaning of this prayer is:

_____

_____

_____

שְׁמַע

יִשְׂרָאֵל

1
אֶחָד

בָּרוּךְ

כָּבֵד

מֶלֶךְ

עֲצֹר!

To Talk About

In the Torah, the שְׁמַע is printed with a large עֹ at the end of the word שְׁמַע and a large ד at the end of the word אֶחָד. There are many different explanations for these large letters. One is that they form the word עֵד, which means "witness."

1. What does it mean to be a witness?

2. What is the connection between saying the שְׁמַע and being a witness?

3. In the Midrash, Shimon bar Yoḥai said that God says:

    "When you are My witness, then I am God. When you are not My witness, then it is as if I am not God."

    Can you explain his idea in your own words?

4. What must we feel and believe to say the שְׁמַע like a witness?

Choreography

When we say the שְׁמַע we do many things to help the words reach our souls and move our hearts.

1. Traditionally, one may stand or sit for the שְׁמַע, but many congregations stand to make it a declaration (like the Pledge of Allegiance).

2. We close our eyes and cover them—so that we are thinking and feeling and not looking around.

3. We make sure that we say every word slowly and clearly, thinking about the meaning.

4. We hold onto the word אֶחָד, making sure that we pronounce the final "ד" so that it will not be mistaken for another word.

עוֹלָם

word parts		words	
us/our = נוּ		our God = אֱלֹהֵינוּ	
to = לְ		name = שֵׁם	
His = וֹ		and more = וָעֶד	
		honor = כְּבוֹד	

71

Reciting Other שְׁמַע Phrases

1. שְׁמַע יִשְׂרָאֵל יי אֱלֹהֵינוּ יי אֶחָד.

2. בָּרוּךְ אַתָּה יי, שׁוֹמֵעַ תְּפִלָּה.

3. כִּי אַתָּה שׁוֹמֵעַ תְּפִלַּת עַמְּךָ יִשְׂרָאֵל בְּרַחֲמִים.

4. וְהָיָה אִם־שָׁמֹעַ תִּשְׁמְעוּ אֶל־מִצְוֹתַי.

5. שָׁמוֹר וְזָכוֹר בְּדִבּוּר אֶחָד, הִשְׁמִיעָנוּ אֵל הַמְיֻחָד.

6. אֲבִינוּ מַלְכֵּנוּ שְׁמַע קוֹלֵנוּ, חוּס וְרַחֵם עָלֵינוּ.

Vocabulary Review

Match the Hebrew word to its English translation.

Match the word to the picture.

love	יִשְׂרָאֵל		שְׁמַע
Israel	בָּרוּךְ		לֶחֶם
mitzvot	מִצְוֹת		לְהַדְלִיק
bless	אַהֲבָה		פְּרִי הַגָּפֶן

72

The Death of Jacob

All of the שְׁמַע is found in the Torah except for one sentence. The part where we say בָּרוּךְ שֵׁם כְּבוֹד מַלְכוּתוֹ לְעוֹלָם וָעֶד is not in there. In most synagogues (but not in many Reform synagogues) this sentence is whispered every day except Yom Kippur. In the Talmud and the Midrash we find three different stories of the origin of the בָּרוּךְ שֵׁם sentence. Two of them also explain the whisper.

Jacob is in Egypt, and he is old and ready to die. Jacob has a second name—at least some of the time he is called יִשְׂרָאֵל. On his deathbed, Jacob gathers his children and tells them, "I am afraid to die."

They answer, "There is no need to fear death, Father. God loves you."

Jacob says, "I am not afraid of dying—I am afraid of leaving you in Egypt without me. Egypt is a land that believes in many gods. Its people carves statues of people out of sides of mountains and pretend that they are gods. I am afraid that when I am gone, you will forget the one God, the God who spoke to Abraham and Isaac and me."

His children answer together in loud voices, "שְׁמַע יִשְׂרָאֵל (Listen, Dad), יי אֱלֹהֵינוּ (Adonai is our God), יי אֶחָד (only Adonai)."

73

With his dying breath Jacob whispers, "בָּרוּךְ הַשֵּׁם (Praised be God) כְּבוֹד מַלְכוּתוֹ לְעוֹלָם וָעֶד (whose glorious empire will last forever)."

When we say the שְׁמַע and whisper the בָּרוּךְ שֵׁם we are acting out this story.

From the Midrash

Questions

1. How is the way we say the שְׁמַע a kind of performance of this story?
2. What were Israel's children promising him? When do you make the same promise?
3. What was Israel's feeling when he said the בָּרוּךְ שֵׁם (and added it to the שְׁמַע)? When have you felt the same way?
4. What is the "Oneness" in this story?
5. How can remembering this story help you point your heart when you say the שְׁמַע?

A Review

Some things to remember about the שְׁמַע

- The שְׁמַע is a quotation from the Torah that was chosen to be the heart of the first part of the morning and evening services.
- The second line, the בָּרוּךְ שֵׁם, was added.
- The whole שְׁמַע is made up of three different paragraphs from the Torah that were brought together to replace a public reading of the Ten Commandments.
- The שְׁמַע states the most important Jewish idea, "There is only one God."

Language Learning

We learned or reviewed the following words:

and more				name			
וָעֶד	עוֹלָם	מֶלֶךְ	כָּבֵד	שֵׁם	אֶחָד	יִשְׂרָאֵל	שְׁמַע

We looked at the following roots  and  ,

 and the prefixes , and the suffixes and .

וְאָהַבְתָּ

The וְאָהַבְתָּ is
- part of the first paragraph of the שְׁמַע,
- the prayer that comes after the שְׁמַע.

It depends how your סִדּוּר is organized. The וְאָהַבְתָּ comes from the book of Deuteronomy, chapter 6, verse 5. The verse before this one is the sentence that begins שְׁמַע יִשְׂרָאֵל.

The וְאָהַבְתָּ continues this idea. It teaches us that
- we should love God,
- the way to show our love is by studying and living Torah,
- מִצְוֹת are the way we live Torah,
- there are מִצְוֹת we can do at all times of the day (every day),
- there are מִצְוֹת we can do anywhere and everywhere we go,
- some Jewish things we do help us to remember the מִצְוֹת,
- teaching Torah to our children is a very important מִצְוָה.

Some congregations say three paragraphs of the שְׁמַע in their service, some say only one. Those that say only one take the last line of the third paragraph and put it on the ending of the וְאָהַבְתָּ. This is the part that tells us that by doing the מִצְוֹת we become קָדוֹשׁ, holy.

In this unit you will learn
- about the first paragraph of the שְׁמַע
- ways of loving God
- two stories about the שְׁמַע

75

וְאָהַבְתָּ

LISTEN, ISRAEL	שְׁמַע יִשְׂרָאֵל 1.
ADONAI is our God, ADONAI is the ONE (and only) God.	יי אֱלֹהֵינוּ יי אֶחָד. 2.
BLESSED be the NAME—that God's HONORED EMPIRE	בָּרוּךְ שֵׁם כְּבוֹד מַלְכוּתוֹ 3.
will last FOREVER and ALWAYS.	לְעוֹלָם וָעֶד. 4.
You should LOVE ADONAI, your God,	וְאָהַבְתָּ אֵת יי אֱלֹהֶיךָ 5.
with all your HEART	בְּכָל-לְבָבְךָ 6.
with all your SOUL	וּבְכָל-נַפְשְׁךָ 7.
with all your STUFF.	וּבְכָל-מְאֹדֶךָ. 8.
And these THINGS that	וְהָיוּ הַדְּבָרִים הָאֵלֶּה 9.
I make MITZVOT for you today	אֲשֶׁר אָנֹכִי מְצַוְּךָ הַיּוֹם 10.
shall be on your HEART.	עַל-לְבָבֶךָ. 11.
You should TEACH them to your children	וְשִׁנַּנְתָּם לְבָנֶיךָ 12.
and you should TALK about them	וְדִבַּרְתָּ בָּם 13.
when you SIT at home	בְּשִׁבְתְּךָ בְּבֵיתֶךָ 14.
when you are GOING out	וּבְלֶכְתְּךָ בַדֶּרֶךְ 15.
when you LIE down	וּבְשָׁכְבְּךָ 16.
and when you get UP.	וּבְקוּמֶךָ 17.
And you should TIE them as LETTERS on your HAND	וּקְשַׁרְתָּם לְאוֹת עַל-יָדֶךָ 18.
And have them as SYMBOLS between your EYES.	וְהָיוּ לְטֹטָפֹת בֵּין עֵינֶיךָ. 19.
And you should WRITE them on the DOORPOSTS of your HOUSE	Uch'tavtam וּכְתַבְתָּם עַל-מְזֻזוֹת בֵּיתֶךָ 20.
and on your GATES.	וּבִשְׁעָרֶיךָ. 21.

Maimonides taught that we find three things in the first paragraph of the שְׁמַע: (1) a statement of our belief that God is one and that God is our ruler, (2) a commitment to completely love God, and (3) a commitment to live a life of Torah. Where in this first paragraph do you find each of these things?

The וְאָהַבְתָּ commands three different kinds of love for God: Heart-love, Soul-love, and Stuff-love. What is the difference between these three kinds of love? Can you give an example of each?

22.	לְמַעַן תִּזְכְּרוּ	That you will REMEMBER
23.	וַעֲשִׂיתֶם אֶת־כָּל־מִצְוֹתָי	and DO all My MITZVOT
24.	וִהְיִיתֶם קְדוֹשִׁים לֵאלֹהֵיכֶם.	and BE HOLY for your God.
25.	אֲנִי יי אֱלֹהֵיכֶם.	I am ADONAI, your God
26.	אֲשֶׁר הוֹצֵאתִי אֶתְכֶם	The One-Who-BROUGHT-you-OUT
27.	מֵאֶרֶץ מִצְרַיִם	from the Land of Egypt
28.	לִהְיוֹת לָכֶם לֵאלֹהִים	to BE your God
29.	אֲנִי יי אֱלֹהֵיכֶם. אֱמֶת.	I am ADONAI, your God. FOR SURE.

מִצְוֹת Found in the שְׁמַע

There are many מִצְוֹת found in the three paragraphs of the שְׁמַע. Can you name them?

The Mitzvot
צִיצִית Tallit
מְזוּזָה Mezuzah
תַּלְמוּד תּוֹרָה Torah Study
תְּפִילִין Tefillin
שְׁמַע עַל מִטָּה Shema at Bedtime
שַׁחֲרִית (Morning) and מַעֲרִיב (Evening) Services

Which of these מִצְוֹת are designed to help you remember the other מִצְוֹת?

אָהַב

all

לֵב

נֶפֶשׁ
Soul

How to Love God

Translate the first line of this prayer.

Your teacher will help you with your translation.

וְאָהַבְתָּ אֵת יְיָ אֱלֹהֶיךָ
בְּכָל־לְבָבְךָ וּבְכָל־נַפְשְׁךָ וּבְכָל־מְאֹדֶךָ.

My best guess at the meaning of this prayer is:

_____

_____

_____

מְאֹד
Stuff

word parts

and = וְ/וּ

your = ךָ

in/with = בְּ

words

before = אֵת
a direct
object

קָמֵץ קָטָן

Sometimes the vowel ָ is pronounced like an ֹ and not an ָ. When that happens, it is called a *kammatz katan*. In this book we will print every ָ *kammatz katan* a little larger than an ordinary ָ, and it will be easier for you to recognize them. Some סִדּוּרִים do this as well.

Kammatz katan means "a short *kammatz*." A regular *kammatz* makes an "ah" sound. A *kammatz katan* makes an "awe" sound. According to people who study languages, an "awe" is a short "ah."

There are some very complicated rules for knowing when to say a *kammatz katan*. A lot of words will become familiar because you will use them often.

Here are two words from the prayer וְאָהַבְתָּ that contain a *kammatz katan*.

עֲצֹר!

וּבְשָׁכְבְּךָ   בְּכָל

Go back to pages 76-77 and practice the וְאָהַבְתָּ before you work on this page.

Some Words Have Endings

Remember the ךָ ending?

ךָ means "your".

שְׁמֶךָ   בְּתוֹרָתֶךָ

Your name   Your Torah

Match the words on the right with the words that have ךָ endings.

אֱלֹהֶיךָ	נֶפֶשׁ
לְבָבְךָ	שְׁעָרִים
נַפְשְׁךָ	לֵב
מְאֹדֶךָ	עֵינַיִם
לְבָנֶיךָ	מְאֹד
יָדֶךָ	אֱלֹהִים
עֵינֶיךָ	בַּיִת
בֵּיתֶךָ	בָּנִים
שְׁעָרֶיךָ	יָד

79

How to Love God 2

בָּנִים

דִּבֵּר

יָשַׁב

בֵּית

הָלַךְ

דֶּרֶךְ

שָׁכַב

Your teacher will help you with your translation of this part of the prayer.

וְשִׁנַּנְתָּם לְבָנֶיךָ וְדִבַּרְתָּ בָּם

בְּשִׁבְתְּךָ בְּבֵיתֶךָ

וּבְלֶכְתְּךָ בַדֶּרֶךְ

וּבְשָׁכְבְּךָ וּבְקוּמֶךָ

My best guess at the meaning of this prayer is:

_____

_____

_____

_____

To Talk About

This part of the שְׁמַע presents two big questions:

(1) It tells us that we should love God by studying Torah all of the time. Does Torah really have something to do with every minute of our lives? Aren't there times that have nothing to do with Torah?

(2) How do we fit Torah into every moment? How do we connect Torah to everything we do?

קוּם

(word parts)

and = וְ/וּ

to = לְ

your = ךָ

in/with = בְּ

(words)

teach them = שִׁנַּנְתָּם

them = בָּם

Moses Steals the שְׁמַע

Moses went up to heaven to get the Torah. All the angels were gathered around him, carrying signs and yelling, "Keep the Torah! Don't let it go!"

Moses took off his *tallit katan,* the little tallit he wore under his robe, and tied it onto his staff. He shouted, "Truce." Four angels came forward to talk to him, Michael, Gavriel, Uzziel, and Raphael. Moses said, "Let me ask three questions. Then you can choose to let me have the Torah, or I will just go home and not bother you anymore."

They said, "We can handle three questions."

Moses asked, "Who here has ever been disrespectful to their parents? Please raise your hand if the answer is 'yes'." All the angels held their hands down.

They said, "We are angels—we don't have parents."

Then Moses asked, "Who has ever stolen something? Please shout out 'Me.'"

The angels were silent. They put their hands over their mouths, and through their fingers they said, "We are angels—we don't steal."

Finally Moses asked, "Who here has ever murdered someone? Please take a step forward."

Every angel took a step back, except one, who stood still. All of the angels said, "We're angels—we don't murder."

Then Moses shouted, "Don't you get it? You don't need the Torah—we do. Torah isn't for those who already do what God wants. Torah is for those of us who need to learn how to be more like God in our actions."

The angels agreed. They shouted out, "Give the Torah to Moses," and they carried him around on their shoulders.

Then the one angel who had not moved, the Angel of Death, came to Moses and whispered three words, "*T'shuvah* (repentence), *t'fillah* (prayer) and *tzedakah* (charity). These are the ways to keep me away."

Just before he left heaven, Moses heard music in the background. He realized that Gavriel and some of the other angels were always filling heaven with songs of praise. One of the songs they were singing over and over went, "בָּרוּךְ שֵׁם כְּבוֹד מַלְכוּתוֹ לְעוֹלָם וָעֶד." Moses stole the angel's song and brought it back to earth along with the Torah.

We now sing the angels' song, "בָּרוּךְ שֵׁם," as part of the שְׁמַע everyday. We whisper it because it was stolen. We say it out loud on Yom Kippur. That is the day by which we have done *t'shuvah*, *t'fillah* and *tzedakah*. It is the one time when we are not guilty of being disrespectful to parents, of stealing, or of murdering. It is the one time that we are as holy as angels.

Based on a story in the Talmud

Questions
1. Why do we usually whisper part of the שְׁמַע?
2. Why do we say it out loud on Yom Kippur?
3. This story teaches us that we are supposed to live the truth that there is only one God by acting the way God wants. What are some of the ways of acting that are on God's list?
4. What is the "Oneness" in this story?
5. How can remembering this story help you point your heart when you say the שְׁמַע?

Go back to pages 76-77 and practice the וְאָהַבְתָּ before you work on this page.

Phrase Drill

Recite these phrases

1. שְׁמַע יִשְׂרָאֵל יי אֱלֹהֵינוּ יי אֶחָד   בָּרוּךְ שֵׁם כְּבוֹד מַלְכוּתוֹ

2. וְשִׁנַּנְתָּם לְבָנֶיךָ וְדִבַּרְתָּ בָּם   וְהָיוּ לְטֹטָפֹת בֵּין עֵינֶיךָ

3. אֲשֶׁר הוֹצֵאתִי אֶתְכֶם מֵאֶרֶץ מִצְרַיִם   וְהָיוּ הַדְּבָרִים הָאֵלֶּה

4. יוֹצֵר אוֹר וּבוֹרֵא חֹשֶׁךְ   חֶמְלָה גְדוֹלָה וִיתֵרָה

5. בְּשִׁבְתְּךָ בְּבֵיתֶךָ וּבְלֶכְתְּךָ בַדֶּרֶךְ   וְהָאֵר עֵינֵינוּ בְּתוֹרָתֶךָ

6. אַהֲבָה רַבָּה אֲהַבְתָּנוּ יי אֱלֹהֵינוּ   וּקְשַׁרְתָּם לְאוֹת עַל יָדֶךָ

7. וּכְתַבְתָּם עַל מְזֻזוֹת בֵּיתֶךָ וּבִשְׁעָרֶיךָ   עֹשֶׂה שָׁלוֹם וּבוֹרֵא אֶת הַכֹּל

8. לְמַעַן תִּזְכְּרוּ וַעֲשִׂיתֶם אֶת כָּל מִצְוֹתָי וִהְיִיתֶם קְדֹשִׁים לֵאלֹהֵיכֶם

9. וַהֲבִיאֵנוּ לְשָׁלוֹם מֵאַרְבַּע כַּנְפוֹת הָאָרֶץ וְתוֹלִיכֵנוּ קוֹמְמִיּוּת לְאַרְצֵנוּ

10. הַמֵּאִיר לָאָרֶץ וְלַדָּרִים עָלֶיהָ   בְּרַחֲמִים וּבְטוּבוֹ מְחַדֵּשׁ בְּכָל-יוֹם תָּמִיד

11. וְתֵן בְּלִבֵּנוּ לְהָבִין וּלְהַשְׂכִּיל לִשְׁמוֹעַ לִלְמֹד וּלְלַמֵּד לִשְׁמֹר וְלַעֲשׂוֹת

12. וְדַבֵּק לִבֵּנוּ בְּמִצְוֹתֶךָ וְיַחֵד לְבָבֵנוּ לְאַהֲבָה וּלְיִרְאָה אֶת שְׁמֶךָ

Ways to Remind Ourselves to Love God

קֶשֶׁר

אוֹתִיּוֹת

יָד

עֵינַיִם

כָּתַב

מְזוּזָה

בַּיִת

Your teacher will help you with your translation of this part of the prayer.

וּקְשַׁרְתָּם לְאוֹת עַל־יָדֶךָ

וְהָיוּ לְטֹטָפֹת בֵּין עֵינֶיךָ.

וּכְתַבְתָּם עַל־מְזֻזוֹת בֵּיתֶךָ וּבִשְׁעָרֶיךָ.

My best guess at the meaning of this prayer is:

_____

_____

_____

To Talk About

The וְאָהַבְתָּ commands "love." It is hard to make a מִצְוָה out of love. "I 'command' that you love me" doesn't quite work—you can't command feelings. But God is smart. Why did God make love a מִצְוָה? Rashi, a famous biblical commentator, said, "God did not command love. God commanded that we do the מִצְוֹת. That is why the Torah says 'These things that I make מִצְוֹת for you today shall be on your heart.' מִצְוֹת are the things we do that teach us to love God and have us pass our love of God on to other people."

Rabbi Levi Yitzhak of Berditchev taught, "Our love of God can be measured in our love of other people." How do you understand the מִצְוָה of loving God?

שַׁעַר

word parts	
and = וְ/וּ	
to = לְ	
your = ךָ	
in/with = בְּ	

words	
on = עַל	
and they shall be = וְהָיוּ	
symbols = טֹטָפוֹת	
between = בֵּין	

The שְׁמַע Rebuilds the Temple

Sometimes a whole story can be told in a sentence. The Temple was the place where the Jewish people came close to God. Three times a year every Jew would come up to Jerusalem, up to the Temple. The Temple was a very big place, but it was not actually big enough to fit all of the Jewish people. We are told that on those days the Temple would stretch to make sure that there was room for everyone.

Here is the one sentence story. Everywhere else in the world Jews answered a prayer with "אָמֵן," but in the Temple, the people answered, "בָּרוּךְ שֵׁם כְּבוֹד מַלְכוּתוֹ לְעוֹלָם וָעֶד."

אָמֵן means "me too." It is a way of saying, "I believe what he or she said." When you say "אָמֵן" God gives you credit for saying the prayer you've heard another person say. When the rabbis added the בָּרוּךְ שֵׁם to the שְׁמַע, they made that one prayer a time when every Jew was again in the Temple. When we say בָּרוּךְ שֵׁם, we know that we are One people—connected to the One God.

Questions
1. What was the original purpose of the בָּרוּךְ שֵׁם?
2. How did it change the שְׁמַע?
3. What is "Oneness" in this story?
4. How can knowing this one-sentence story help you point your heart when you say the שְׁמַע?

85

Latifa Kropf told this story. A boy comes to his teacher, Mimi Feigelson, and starts to cry. She asks him what is wrong, and he explains that he has been praying and praying for the Temple to be rebuilt. He is upset that his prayers did not work, the Temple remains broken.

He says, "God doesn't answer me."

The teacher asks the boy to close his eyes. She says, "Imagine that the Temple has become whole."

The boy closes his eyes, and slowly a great smile fills his face. Finally he opens his eyes and says, "Teacher, I saw it—I really saw it—the Temple whole."

The teacher smiles at him and says, "Your prayers were answered."

Questions

1. How was the Temple made whole?
2. How is the בָּרוּךְ שֵׁם in the שְׁמַע the same as the closed eyes in this story?

עֲצֹר!

Comparing the Two Versions

A. שְׁמַע יִשְׂרָאֵל

B. יי אֱלֹהֵינוּ יי אֶחָד.

בָּרוּךְ שֵׁם כְּבוֹד מַלְכוּתוֹ לְעוֹלָם וָעֶד.

C. וְאָהַבְתָּ אֵת יי אֱלֹהֶיךָ

D. בְּכָל־לְבָבְךָ וּבְכָל־נַפְשְׁךָ וּבְכָל־מְאֹדֶךָ.

E. וְהָיוּ הַדְּבָרִים הָאֵלֶּה

F. אֲשֶׁר אָנֹכִי מְצַוְּךָ הַיּוֹם עַל־לְבָבֶךָ.

G. וְשִׁנַּנְתָּם לְבָנֶיךָ וְדִבַּרְתָּ בָּם

H. בְּשִׁבְתְּךָ בְּבֵיתֶךָ וּבְלֶכְתְּךָ בַדֶּרֶךְ

I. וּבְשָׁכְבְּךָ וּבְקוּמֶךָ.

J. וּקְשַׁרְתָּם לְאוֹת עַל־יָדֶךָ

K. וְהָיוּ לְטֹטָפֹת בֵּין עֵינֶיךָ.

L. וּכְתַבְתָּם עַל־מְזֻזוֹת בֵּיתֶךָ וּבִשְׁעָרֶיךָ.

1. וְהָיָה אִם־שָׁמֹעַ תִּשְׁמְעוּ אֶל־מִצְוֹתַי

2. אֲשֶׁר אָנֹכִי מְצַוֶּה אֶתְכֶם הַיּוֹם

3. לְאַהֲבָה אֶת־יי אֱלֹהֵיכֶם וּלְעָבְדוֹ

4. בְּכָל־לְבַבְכֶם וּבְכָל־נַפְשְׁכֶם

5. וְנָתַתִּי מְטַר־אַרְצְכֶם בְּעִתּוֹ

6. יוֹרֶה וּמַלְקוֹשׁ

7. וְאָסַפְתָּ דְגָנֶךָ וְתִירֹשְׁךָ וְיִצְהָרֶךָ.

8. וְנָתַתִּי עֵשֶׂב בְּשָׂדְךָ לִבְהֶמְתֶּךָ

9. וְאָכַלְתָּ וְשָׂבָעְתָּ.

10. הִשָּׁמְרוּ לָכֶם פֶּן־יִפְתֶּה לְבַבְכֶם

11. וְסַרְתֶּם וַעֲבַדְתֶּם אֱלֹהִים אֲחֵרִים

12. וְהִשְׁתַּחֲוִיתֶם לָהֶם

13. וְחָרָה אַף־יי בָּכֶם

14. וְעָצַר אֶת־הַשָּׁמַיִם וְלֹא־יִהְיֶה מָטָר

15. וְהָאֲדָמָה לֹא תִתֵּן אֶת־יְבוּלָהּ

16. וַאֲבַדְתֶּם מְהֵרָה מֵעַל הָאָרֶץ הַטֹּבָה

17. אֲשֶׁר יי נֹתֵן לָכֶם

18. וְשַׂמְתֶּם אֶת־דְּבָרַי אֵלֶּה

19. עַל־לְבַבְכֶם וְעַל־נַפְשְׁכֶם

20. וּקְשַׁרְתֶּם אֹתָם לְאוֹת עַל־יֶדְכֶם

21. וְהָיוּ לְטוֹטָפֹת בֵּין עֵינֵיכֶם.

22. וְלִמַּדְתֶּם אֹתָם אֶת־בְּנֵיכֶם לְדַבֵּר בָּם

23. בְּשִׁבְתְּךָ בְּבֵיתֶךָ וּבְלֶכְתְּךָ בַדֶּרֶךְ

24. וּבְשָׁכְבְּךָ וּבְקוּמֶךָ

25. וּכְתַבְתָּם עַל־מְזוּזוֹת בֵּיתֶךָ וּבִשְׁעָרֶיךָ.

26. לְמַעַן יִרְבּוּ יְמֵיכֶם

27. וִימֵי בְנֵיכֶם עַל הָאֲדָמָה

28. אֲשֶׁר נִשְׁבַּע יי לַאֲבֹתֵיכֶם לָתֵת לָהֶם

29. כִּימֵי הַשָּׁמַיִם עַל הָאָרֶץ.

Comparing the Two Versions

The second paragraph of the שְׁמַע is very much like the first paragraph. There is only big difference. In the first paragraph, Moses is talking to individual Jews. It is in the singular. It is a one-Jew-at-a-time teaching of the relationship between God and Israel.

The second paragraph of the שְׁמַע (Deuteronomy 11:13-21) is Moses talking to the Jewish people as a whole. This one is written in the plural. This paragraph is about the collective relationship between Israel and God.

See if you can match the similar parts of the two versions. Look for the words you know. Look at the roots you know. You will find the same phrases but the words may have slightly different endings.

Why do we need both a singular and a plural version of this text?

Go back to pages 76-77 and practice the וְאָהַבְתָּ before you work on this word search.

וְאָהַבְתָּ Word Search

ת	וֹ	ז	זֻ	מְ	יָ	שְׁ
ךָ	וְּ	צַ	מְ	בָּ	דֶ	מַ
יִ	נַ	וְ	אֹ	ם	ךָ	ע
שְׁ	פְ	אָ	דֶ	ד	חָ	אֶ
ךָ	שְׁ	הַ	ךָ	בְ	בַ	לְ
אֵ	ךָ	בְ	ה	לֶ	אֵ	הָ
ל	ם	תָּ	נְ	נַּ	שׁ	וְ

Find the following words in this word search:

יָדֶךָ שְׁמַע הָאֵלֶּה

אֶחָד וְאָהַבְתָּ וְשִׁנַּנְתָּם

מְצַוְּךָ מְזֻזוֹת נַפְשְׁךָ

לְבָבְךָ יִשְׂרָאֵל מְאֹדֶךָ

A Review

Some things to remember about the וְאָהַבְתָּ

- The וְאָהַבְתָּ is part of the first paragraph of the שְׁמַע.
- The וְאָהַבְתָּ teaches us how to love God. It tells us that we can grow our love for God and show our love for God by studying Torah and performing מִצְוֹת.
- The וְאָהַבְתָּ is the source for many Jewish practices, including praying morning and evening services, saying the שְׁמַע at bedtime, wearing תְּפִילִּין, putting up a מְזוּזָה, and studying Torah. Wearing a טַלִּית comes from the third paragraph of the שְׁמַע.

Language Learning

Some of the words we learned or reviewed in this lesson are:

שַׁעַר

אוֹתִיּוֹת

דֶּרֶךְ

בָּנִים

teach them
וְשִׁנַּנְתָּם

stuff
מְאֹד

soul
נֶפֶשׁ

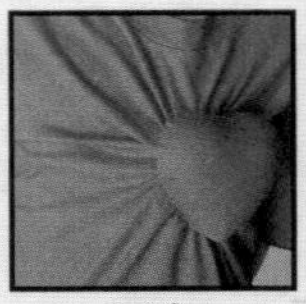
לֵב

We reviewed the roots שמע and אהב, prefixes בְּ, לְ, וְ/וּ, and suffixes ךָ, וֹ.

מִי-כָמֹכָה

The מִי-כָמֹכָה is

- a sentence out of a poem in the Torah,
- part of the song that the Families-of-Israel sang when they crossed the Reed Sea,
- part of the בְּרָכָה that comes after שְׁמַע in both the morning and the evening,
- a reminder that God has helped us and will continue to help us.

When the Families-of-Israel escaped from Egypt, the Egyptians chased them and caught up with them at the Reed Sea. (Reed Sea is what the Hebrew actually says. "Red" Sea is a typo.) God worked a miracle and the sea divided so that Israel crossed it safely on dry land. When the Egyptians tried to follow, the sea closed up, and they drowned. Once they were safely on the other side (or maybe even before) Israel burst into song. The song they sang, the Song of the Sea, includes מִי-כָמֹכָה.

The third prayer connected to the שְׁמַע, the one that comes after the שְׁמַע, is called the גְּאֻלָה, which means "redemption." Redemption is a combination of rescuing and setting free. God redeemed us from Egyptian slavery. That is why this בְּרָכָה ends by saying

בָּרוּךְ אַתָּה יי גָּאַל יִשְׂרָאֵל.

In this unit you will learn
- about מִי-כָמֹכָה
- about the Golem
- three stories about crossing the Reed Sea.

89

גְּאֻלָּה

Moses and the Families-of-Israel	מֹשֶׁה וּבְנֵי יִשְׂרָאֵל 1.
responded to You in very happy song	לְךָ עָנוּ שִׁירָה בְּשִׂמְחָה רַבָּה, 2.
and they all said:	וְאָמְרוּ כֻלָּם: 3.
Which of the other (false) gods is like You, ADONAI	מִי־כָמֹכָה בָּאֵלִים יְיָ, 4.
Who is like You, GLORIOUS in holiness	מִי כָּמֹכָה נֶאְדָּר בַּקֹּדֶשׁ, 5.
AWESOME in praises, DOING miracles?	נוֹרָא תְהִלֹּת עֹשֵׂה פֶלֶא. 6.
With a new song the REDEEMED proclaimed Your Name	שִׁירָה חֲדָשָׁה שִׁבְּחוּ גְאוּלִים לְשִׁמְךָ 7.
on the sea shore.	עַל שְׂפַת הַיָּם, 8.
Together all of them gave thanks and praised Your Empire	יַחַד כֻּלָּם הוֹדוּ וְהִמְלִיכוּ 9.
by saying:	וְאָמְרוּ: 10.
ADONAI will rule forever and ever.	יְיָ יִמְלֹךְ לְעֹלָם וָעֶד. 11.
Rock of Israel,	צוּר יִשְׂרָאֵל 12.
Arise in help of Israel	קוּמָה בְּעֶזְרַת יִשְׂרָאֵל, 13.
and set (us) free,	וּפְדֵה 14.
as You promised to JUDAH and ISRAEL,	כִנְאֻמֶךָ יְהוּדָה וְיִשְׂרָאֵל. 15.
and REDEEM us.	גֹּאֲלֵנוּ 16.
ADONAI of Hosts is God's NAME, holy is Israel.	יְיָ צְבָאוֹת שְׁמוֹ קְדוֹשׁ יִשְׂרָאֵל. 17.
BLESSED be You, ADONAI,	בָּרוּךְ אַתָּה יְיָ 18.
The ONE-Who-REDEEMED Israel.	גָּאַל יִשְׂרָאֵל. 19.

I do this

1. In the Jerusalem Talmud we are told, "Part of saying the שְׁמַע in the morning is the obligation to remember the Exodus." The גְּאֻלָּה is the way we fulfill that obligation. Why do you think that the memory of the Exodus is needed to complete the שְׁמַע?

2. Moses and the Families-of-Israel sang the Song of the Sea responsively. That is exactly the way we pray the מִי־כָמֹכָה. The leader sings a line and then we respond. Praying the מִי־כָמֹכָה is reliving the Exodus. It is remembering being redeemed by God.

True and Certain

This is the first sentence of the גְּאֻלָּה. Read through this part and make your best guess at its meaning.

loved	believable	straight	established	correct	certain	true
וְאָהוּב	וְנֶאֱמָן,	וְיָשָׁר,	וְקַיָם	וְנָכוֹן,	וְיַצִּיב,	אֱמֶת,

1.

sweet	splendid	awesome	nice	pleasant	cherished
וּמְתֻקָּן	וְאַדִּיר,	וְנוֹרָא	וְנָעִים	וְנֶחְמָד,	וְחָבִיב,

2.

forever		on us	this	thing	beautiful	good	acceptable
וָעֶד.	לְעוֹלָם	עָלֵינוּ	הַזֶּה	הַדָּבָר	וְיָפֶה	וְטוֹב,	וּמְקֻבָּל,

3.

My best guess at the meaning of this prayer is:

_____

_____

_____

_____

Your teacher will help you sort these words into a translation.

To Talk about

The rabbis of the Talmud said that God had many names, and אֱמֶת was one of them. What lesson can we learn from the fact that אֱמֶת is one of God's names?

What are some true things you can say about God?

To understand this picture, sneak ahead to the story on page 92.

The Golem

The Jews of Prague were in lots of danger. Some of the non-Jews in the town were telling lies about them and making many people angry. There was danger of a riot against the Jews, called a pogrom.

The Chief Rabbi of Prague was Judah Lowe. He was a great scholar, and he was a student of the Kabbalah, the mysteries of the Torah. One night he took his best student and his assistant down to the riverbank. They spent hours shaping a man out of river mud. Judah Lowe said prayers, and he put a piece of paper with the secret seventy-two-letter name of God into the mud man's mouth. Last, he traced three letters on the mud man's forehead—the first letter of the Alef-Bet, an א; the middle letter, a מ; and the last letter, a ת. The three letters spelled one of God's names, אֱמֶת. Slowly, the mud man came alive. He became Joseph Golem, who was like a person, but was extra strong and could not talk.

The Golem protected Prague. He stopped many people who were trying to frame the Jews by planting false evidence in the Ghetto. He protected the Jews from those who would attack them. In the end, the Golem showed the world who were the real liars.

When the danger had passed, Rabbi Lowe erased the letter א from the Golem's forehead, and he became mud once more. The remaining two letters spelled מֵת, the Hebrew word for death.

A Folk Tale

עֲצֹר!

Questions

1. Why do you think the word אֱמֶת helped to bring the Golem to life?
2. How can knowing this story help you point your heart when you say the מִי־כָמֹכָה?

92

Go back to page 90 and practice the גְּאֻלָּה before you work on this page.

מִי־כָמֹכָה בָּאֵלִים יי
מִי כָּמֹכָה נֶאְדָּר בַּקֹּדֶשׁ
נוֹרָא תְהִלֹּת עֹשֵׂה פֶלֶא

My best guess at the meaning of this prayer is:

_____

_____

To Talk About

מִי־כָמֹכָה praises God for rescuing Israel and for punishing the Egyptian army. In the Midrash we learn that the destruction of the Egyptians bothered God. We are told that while Israel sang God's praises on earth, the angels were joining in up in heaven. But God said to them, "Stop singing! My children are drowning."

Who were God's children in this story? Why did God stop the angels from singing? Why did God let Israel continue singing? What can this story teach you about praying the מִי־כָמֹכָה?

Your teacher will help you with your translation.

word parts	words	
your = ךָ	awesome = נוֹרָא	who = מִי
in/with = בְּ/בַּ/בָ	praises = תְהִלֹּת	is like = כָּמוֹ
	do/make = עֹשֵׂה	gods = אֵלִים
	wonder = פֶלֶא	splendor = נֶאְדָּר
		holy = קֹדֶשׁ

The Dagesh

A. Name these Hebrew letters: פּ כּ כ בּ ב

B. The dot found inside the letters **פּ**, **כּ** and **בּ** is called a *dagesh*. What does the *dagesh* do to these letters?

_____

C. The *dagesh* can also be found in many other Hebrew letters, but it doesn't change the way the other letters are pronounced.

Circle the letters whose sounds are changed by the dagesh:

1. קּ סּ פּ שּׁ הּ בּ גּ מּ לּ דּ

2. בּ לּ שּׁ נּ טּ יּ צּ כּ זּ

Recite these words from the מִי־כָמֹכָה.

1. פֶּלֶא כָּמֹכָה קַיָּם נָעִים עֹשֵׂה בָּאֵלִים אֱמֶת

2. לְעֹלָם מִי תְהִלֹּת אָהוּב יִמְלֹךְ נוֹרָא נֶאְדָּר

3. וְנוֹרָא בַּקֹּדֶשׁ יַצִּיב חָבִיב תְהִלֹּת נֶאֱמָן וָעֶד

4. כָּמֹכָה נֶחְמָד יָשָׁר נֶאֱמָן אַדִּיר מְתֻקָּן כָּמֹכָה

Recite these phrases from the מִי־כָמֹכָה.

5. מִי כָמֹכָה נֶאְדָּר בַּקֹּדֶשׁ   נוֹרָא תְהִלֹּת עֹשֵׂה פֶלֶא

6. מִי־כָמֹכָה בָּאֵלִים יי   יי יִמְלֹךְ לְעֹלָם וָעֶד

94

Nahshon's Leap of Faith

Here is one of many stories about the first time the מִי־כָמֹכָה was said.

Israel was trapped at the banks of the Reed Sea. The Egyptian army was coming, and there was nowhere to run. Everyone was in a panic. No one knew how to swim well enough. It was a mob scene. God was supposed to rescue them, but nothing was happening. One man, Nahshon ben Aminadav, from the tribe of Judah, figured out the answer. He found himself a little space, backed up, and took a running leap toward the sea. He jumped way out into the water, but he never got wet. When his toe got to a place where it should have touched the water, the sea divided under him and he landed on dry land. Israel could then march forward into the dry sea bed.

From the Midrash

Questions

1. What did Nahshon figure out about what God wants from us?
2. What is the lesson of this midrash?
3. How can remembering the story of Nahshon help us to point our hearts when we say the מִי־כָמֹכָה?

עֲצֹר!

95

מֶלֶךְ

עוֹלָם

words

and more = וָעֶד

word parts

to = לְ

Go back to page 90 and practice the גְּאֻלָּה before you work on this page.

Your teacher will help you with your translation.

יי יִמְלֹךְ לְעֹלָם וָעֶד.

My best guess at the meaning of this prayer is:

_____

_____

_____

To Talk About

יי יִמְלֹךְ is the last line in the Song of the Sea. It is the conclusion that Israel reached after they were successfully led out of Egypt. What did they know then that was hard for them to realize when they were still slaves in Egypt?

96

Up Close and Personal with Miriam

After the Families-of-Israel crossed the sea, two song leaders led them in song. One was Moses and the other was Miriam. Miriam was Moses' older sister, the one who watched over him when he was in the ark made out of bulrushes. Miriam was a prophetess, the one who predicted that Moses would lead Israel out of Egypt.

In the wilderness, Israel was kept alive by two things. One was the manna that Moses arranged to have God drop from heaven. The other was Miriam's well, a well that moved from place to place and made sure that Israel always had water. The story of Miriam's well is found in the Midrash.

For forty years, the Families-of Israel had three leaders: Moses, Moses' brother Aaron, and Miriam.

When the Families-of-Israel had safely crossed the Reed Sea, Miriam started to sing, and all the women picked up drums and began to sing and dance with her. The midrash asks an interesting question: Where did the drums come from? The midrash answers its own question by saying, "The women had faith. They believed that God would indeed liberate them from Egypt. They also knew that when God liberated them, they would have to thank and praise God. The women brought the drums as an act of faith. They had already planned that celebration."

When have you been like Miriam and the women, believing in something that seemed almost impossible?

_____

_____

_____

How does knowing the story of Miriam and the women help you to point your heart when you sing the מִי־כָמֹכָה?

_____

_____

_____

The Women Hold Hands

Here is another story of how the Reed Sea divided. Every tribe wanted to be the first to enter the water. Each tribe wanted the bragging rights, so they prevented every other tribe from getting wet. It looked like a huge rugby game with everyone pushing and holding each other back. While the men were busy struggling, the women looked at each other. They nodded and stepped back a little. They took each other's hands and worked their way around the men. They counted together, and on the count of three the women-of-Israel stepped into the sea all at once. The second they entered, the sea divided. When that happened, the men stopped struggling with each other and all of Israel began to cross.

From the Midrash

Questions

1. What did the women figure out about what God wants from us?
2. What is the lesson of this midrash?
3. How can remembering the story of the women help us to point our hearts when we say the מִי־כָמֹכָה?

עֲצֹר!

98

Go back to page 90 and practice the גְּאֻלָה before you work on this page.

Your teacher will help you with your translation.

צוּר יִשְׂרָאֵל, קוּמָה בְּעֶזְרַת יִשְׂרָאֵל,
וּפְדֵה כִנְאֻמֶךָ יְהוּדָה וְיִשְׂרָאֵל,
גֹּאֲלֵנוּ יי צְבָאוֹת שְׁמוֹ קְדוֹשׁ יִשְׂרָאֵל
בָּרוּךְ אַתָּה יי גָּאַל יִשְׂרָאֵל.

> My best guess at the meaning of this prayer is:

_____

_____

_____

_____

_____

_____

צוּר

יִשְׂרָאֵל

קוּם

words

help = עֱזֶר

release = פְּדָה

promise = נְאֻם

Judah = יְהוּדָה

Hosts = צְבָאוֹת

name = שֵׁם

redeem = גְּאַל

word parts

and = וְ/וּ

in/with = בְּ

us/our = נוּ

as/like = כְּ

his = וֹ

your = ךָ

To Talk About

Three בְּרָכוֹת surround the שְׁמַע every morning. The first, יוֹצֵר אוֹר, describes creation in the present tense. The second, אַהֲבָה רַבָּה, talks about revelation in the present tense. The גְּאֻלָה is the third; it talks about redemption in the past tense. Why do you think that the first two are in the present, while the גְּאֻלָה remains in the past?

How to Dance the גְּאֻלָה

It is a tradition to connect the end of the גְּאֻלָה directly, without a pause, to the עֲמִידָה, the chain of prayers that follows. The last sentence of the גְּאֻלָה includes the word קוּמָה at the beginning. קוּמָה means "rise up." It is a tradition to rise up when you say the word קוּמָה and remain standing for the עֲמִידָה that follows.

99

Saying ב with a Mouth Full of Water

 ere is another story of the first time that Israel said the מִי־כָמֹכָה. To understand this story you need to look at the words of the מִי־כָמֹכָה.

מִי־כָמֹכָה בָּאֵלִם יי, מִי כָּמֹכָה נֶאְדָּר בַּקֹּדֶשׁ, נוֹרָא תְהִלֹּת עֹשֵׂה פֶלֶא.

כָמֹכָה is spelled with a כ the first time. It is כָּמֹכָה with a כ the second time.

Israel entered the Reed Sea singing together. When they sang מִי, the water was up to their ankles. The word בָּאֵלִם came as they moved forward and the water reached their waists. By יי the water was at their chests. They were getting nervous, and so they sang more slowly. When they sang the second מִי, the water was up to their necks. Still they pushed on and tried to sing כָּמֹכָה. By the second כָמֹכָה, the water was over their heads. It came out as כָמֹכָה, because you can't say a כָּ when your mouth is full of water. Only when they were in over their heads did God divide the sea.

From the Midrash

Questions

1. What does this story teach us about what God expects from us?
2. What is the lesson of this midrash?
3. How can remembering the story of the water over our heads help us to point our hearts when we say the מִי־כָמֹכָה?

100

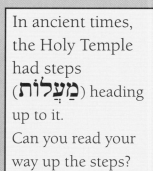

In ancient times, the Holy Temple had steps (מַעֲלוֹת) heading up to it. Can you read your way up the steps?

9. יי יִמְלֹךְ לְעוֹלָם וָעֶד.

8. שְׁמַע יִשְׂרָאֵל יי אֱלֹהֵינוּ יי אֶחָד

7. בָּרוּךְ שֵׁם כְּבוֹד מַלְכוּתוֹ לְעוֹלָם וָעֶד.

6. מִי־כָמֹכָה בָּאֵלִים יי מִי כָּמֹכָה נֶאְדָּר בַּקֹּדֶשׁ

5. וְהָאֵר עֵינֵינוּ בְּתוֹרָתֶךָ וְדַבֵּק לִבֵּנוּ בְּמִצְוֹתֶיךָ

4. אֱמֶת, וְיַצִּיב, וְנָכוֹן, וְקַיָּם, וְיָשָׁר, וְנֶאֱמָן, וְאָהוּב וְחָבִיב

3. וְשִׁנַּנְתָּם לְבָנֶיךָ וְדִבַּרְתָּ בָּם, בְּשִׁבְתְּךָ בְּבֵיתֶךָ וּבְלֶכְתְּךָ בַדֶּרֶךְ

2. וְאָהַבְתָּ אֵת־יי אֱלֹהֶיךָ, בְּכָל־לְבָבְךָ וּבְכָל־נַפְשְׁךָ וּבְכָל־מְאֹדֶךָ

1. צוּר יִשְׂרָאֵל קוּמָה בְּעֶזְרַת יִשְׂרָאֵל, וּפְדֵה כִנְאֻמֶךָ יְהוּדָה וְיִשְׂרָאֵל

START

A Review

Some things to remember about the גְּאֻלָה

- The מִי־כָמֹכָה is part of a larger בְּרָכָה called the גְּאֻלָה. That means "redemption."

- Redemption means "being saved and set free". The prayer is based on the Jews' experience of being redeemed from slavery in Egypt. The מִי־כָמֹכָה is part of the song that the Jewish people sang when they crossed the Reed Sea. We find it in the book of Exodus.

- The מִי־כָמֹכָה is both a past tense and future tense prayer. It reminds us that God has helped us in the past and will again help us in the future. God is our Redeemer.

Language Learning

Some of the words we learned or reviewed in this lesson were:

redeem						is like	who
גָּאַל	קוּם	יִשְׂרָאֵל	צוּר	מֶלֶךְ	קֹדֶשׁ	כְּמוֹ	מִי

Prayer Parts

We looked at four short parts of the גְּאֻלָה and the first sentence that begins with אֱמֶת:

- the מִי־כָמֹכָה,

- the response יי יִמְלֹךְ לְעֹלָם וָעֶד,

- the last part of the prayer, צוּר יִשְׂרָאֵל which includes the final blessing בָּרוּךְ אַתָּה יי גָּאַל יִשְׂרָאֵל.

עֲצֹר!

קִדּוּשׁ

The קִדּוּשׁ is a prayer that welcomes the holiness of שַׁבָּת or a holiday. The קִדּוּשׁ is actually made up of two בְּרָכוֹת.

- One is the בְּרָכָה that is said over the wine, grape juice, or other liquid (anything except water).

- The other is a בְּרָכָה over שַׁבָּת (or the holiday).

You can't hold שַׁבָּת in your hand. You can't taste it or smell it, see it or hear it. שַׁבָּת is not concrete. We say a בְּרָכָה over wine that we can smell, taste, see, and hold in our hand. We add the בְּרָכָה for שַׁבָּת to it.

The Talmud tells us that we have to say the wine בְּרָכָה before the בְּרָכָה for שַׁבָּת. The Talmud compares the wine בְּרָכָה to a friend we see every day and the בְּרָכָה over שַׁבָּת to a Queen. One might want to say hello to a Queen first and then realize that a friend is in the room, but that would be rude. The Talmud wants us to celebrate the everyday first and then look at the special. That is why the wine בְּרָכָה comes before the בְּרָכָה for שַׁבָּת.

The בְּרָכָה over שַׁבָּת teaches two big ideas:

- we celebrate שַׁבָּת because God created the world and then rested,

- we celebrate שַׁבָּת because we were slaves in Egypt and God liberated us.

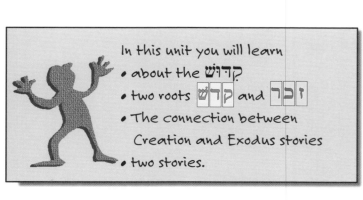

In this unit you will learn
- about the קִדּוּשׁ
- two roots קדשׁ and זכר
- The connection between Creation and Exodus stories
- two stories.

קִדּוּשׁ

Blessed be You, Adonai	בָּרוּךְ אַתָּה יי	1.
our God, Ruler-of-the-Cosmos	אֱלֹהֵינוּ מֶלֶךְ הָעוֹלָם	2.
The ONE-Who-Creates the fruit of the vine.	בּוֹרֵא פְּרִי הַגָּפֶן.	3.
BLESSED are You, the Eternal	בָּרוּךְ אַתָּה יי	4.
our God, Ruler-of-the-Cosmos	אֱלֹהֵינוּ מֶלֶךְ הָעוֹלָם	5.
The ONE-Who-Made us HOLY through the mitzvot	אֲשֶׁר קִדְּשָׁנוּ בְּמִצְוֹתָיו	6.
and the ONE-Who-is pleased with us.	וְרָצָה בָנוּ	7.
And the ONE-Who-gave us the holy Shabbat	וְשַׁבַּת קָדְשׁוֹ	8.
with love and satisfaction	בְּאַהֲבָה וּבְרָצוֹן הִנְחִילָנוּ	9.
as a remembrance of the work of CREATION.	זִכָּרוֹן לְמַעֲשֵׂה בְרֵאשִׁית.	10.
Because this is a day of HALLELUJAH	כִּי הוּא יוֹם תְּחִלָּה	11.
a HOLY time	לְמִקְרָאֵי-קֹדֶשׁ	12.
remembering the EXODUS from Egypt.	זֵכֶר לִיצִיאַת מִצְרָיִם.	13.
Because You chose us	כִּי בָנוּ בָחַרְתָּ	14.
and separated us from all other peoples	וְאוֹתָנוּ קִדַּשְׁתָּ מִכָּל הָעַמִּים	15.
and intentionally separated Shabbat with love	וְשַׁבַּת קָדְשְׁךָ בְּאַהֲבָה וּבְרָצוֹן	16.
as our inheritance.	הִנְחַלְתָּנוּ	17.
Blessed be You, Adonai	בָּרוּךְ אַתָּה יי	18.
The ONE-Who-Makes Shabbat HOLY.	מְקַדֵּשׁ הַשַּׁבָּת.	19.

The traditional קִדּוּשׁ says, "כִּי בָנוּ בָחַרְתָּ וְאוֹתָנוּ קִדַּשְׁתָּ מִכָּל הָעַמִּים" (because You chose us and You set us apart from among all people). This is an expression of the idea of the "Chosen People". In the Reconstructionist Siddur you find instead the words "כִּי אֵלֶינוּ קָרָאתָ וְאוֹתָנוּ קִדַּשְׁתָּ לַעֲבוֹדָתֶךָ" (because You called to us, and You made us holy through Your work). This is an expression of the idea of the "Choosing People". What is the difference between these two ideas? Which one is closer to what you believe?

Review of the root קדש

Do you remember the root קדש, which means "holy"?

holy = קָדוֹשׁ

makes holy = מְקַדֵּשׁ

made us holy = קִדְּשָׁנוּ

Here are some phrases with the root קדש.

1. בָּרוּךְ אַתָּה יי הָאֵל הַקָּדוֹשׁ.

2. קִדְּשָׁנוּ בְּמִצְוֹתֶיךָ וְתֵן חֶלְקֵנוּ בְּתוֹרָתֶךָ.

3. וְשַׁבַּת קָדְשׁוֹ בְּאַהֲבָה וּבְרָצוֹן הִנְחַלְתָּנוּ.

4. אֲשֶׁר קִדְּשָׁנוּ בְּמִצְוֹתָיו וְרָצָה בָנוּ וְשַׁבַּת קָדְשׁוֹ בְּאַהֲבָה וּבְרָצוֹן.

5. קָדוֹשׁ, קָדוֹשׁ, קָדוֹשׁ, יי צְבָאוֹת, מְלֹא כָל-הָאָרֶץ כְּבוֹדוֹ.

6. אַתָּה קָדוֹשׁ וְשִׁמְךָ קָדוֹשׁ, וּקְדוֹשִׁים בְּכָל-יוֹם יְהַלְלוּךָ סֶּלָה.

7. כִּי בְשֵׁם קָדְשְׁךָ הַגָּדוֹל וְהַנּוֹרָא בָּטַחְנוּ, נָגִילָה וְנִשְׂמְחָה בִּישׁוּעָתֶךָ.

8. גְּאָלֵנוּ יי צְבָאוֹת שְׁמוֹ קְדוֹשׁ יִשְׂרָאֵל. בָּרוּךְ אַתָּה יי גָּאַל יִשְׂרָאֵל.

9. נְקַדֵּשׁ אֶת שִׁמְךָ בָּעוֹלָם, כְּשֵׁם שֶׁמַּקְדִּישִׁים אוֹתוֹ בִּשְׁמֵי מָרוֹם.

בָּרוּךְ

אַתָּה

מֶלֶךְ

פְּרִי הַגָּפֶן

קָדוֹשׁ

שַׁבָּת

עֲצֹר!

Your teacher will help you with your translation.

בָּרוּךְ אַתָּה יי אֱלֹהֵינוּ מֶלֶךְ הָעוֹלָם בּוֹרֵא פְּרִי הַגָּפֶן.

בָּרוּךְ אַתָּה יי אֱלֹהֵינוּ מֶלֶךְ הָעוֹלָם

אֲשֶׁר קִדְּשָׁנוּ בְּמִצְוֹתָיו...

בָּרוּךְ אַתָּה יי מְקַדֵּשׁ הַשַּׁבָּת.

My best guess at the meaning of this prayer is:

_____

_____

_____

_____

word parts		words
in/with = בְּ	us/our = נוּ	creates = בּוֹרֵא
	to = לְ	that/which/who = אֲשֶׁר
	the = הַ	His commandments = מִצְוֹתָיו

קִדּוּשׁ Choreography

There are a lot of different קִדּוּשׁ customs.

• Some people stand to make קִדּוּשׁ and some sit. Some people say the קִדּוּשׁ while standing and then sit to actually drink.

• It is a tradition to hold the קִדּוּשׁ cup in your right hand. Some people wrap their fingers around the cup (the usual way to hold it). Some people hold it from underneath—making their hand into a container that holds the wine container.

• One person leads the קִדּוּשׁ. Usually everyone else joins in starting at כִּי בָנוּ בָחַרְתָּ.

Here is a root to remember.

The root זכר means "remember."

זוֹכֵר = remembers

זָכְרֵנוּ = remember us

זִכָּרוֹן = remembrance

Here are some phrases with the root זכר.

1. בָּרוּךְ אַתָּה יי אֱלֹהֵינוּ מֶלֶךְ הָעוֹלָם זוֹכֵר הַבְּרִית

2. זָכְרֵנוּ לְחַיִּים מֶלֶךְ חָפֵץ בַּחַיִּים   זָכוֹר אֶת-יוֹם הַשַּׁבָּת לְקַדְּשׁוֹ

3. וַתִּתֶּן לָנוּ יי אֱלֹהֵינוּ בְּאַהֲבָה אֶת יוֹם הַזִּכָּרוֹן הַזֶּה

4. יוֹם שַׁבָּתוֹן אֵין לִשְׁכּוֹחַ, זִכְרוֹ כְּרֵיחַ הַנִּיחֹחַ

5. כִּי הוּא יוֹם תְּחִלָּה לְמִקְרָאֵי-קֹדֶשׁ זֵכֶר לִיצִיאַת מִצְרָיִם

6. וְשַׁבַּת קָדְשׁוֹ בְּאַהֲבָה וּבְרָצוֹן הִנְחִילָנוּ זִכָּרוֹן לְמַעֲשֵׂה בְרֵאשִׁית

Write in the missing letters for these words built from the root זכר.

Go back to page 104 and practice the קדוש after you work on this page.

7. זָ__וֹר

8. __כָּרוֹן

9. זָכְ__נוּ

10. __כְרוֹ

11. זֵכֶ__

12. יִזְ__ר

107

Your teacher will help you with your translation.

יָצָא

מִצְרַיִם

זָכַר

word parts

לְ = to

words

מַעֲשֶׂה = makings

בְּרֵאשִׁית = creation

To Talk About

Look at these two phrases. The קִדּוּשׁ is built around them.

זִכָּרוֹן לְמַעֲשֶׂה בְרֵאשִׁית.
זֵכֶר לִיצִיאַת מִצְרָיִם.

What is the connection between שַׁבָּת and creation? Why is שַׁבָּת a good way of remembering that God created the world? Why is remembering that God is the Creator a good reason for observing שַׁבָּת?

What is the connection between the Exodus from Egypt and שַׁבָּת? Why is שַׁבָּת a good way of celebrating the Exodus? Why is remembering the Exodus a good reason for observing שַׁבָּת?

זִכָּרוֹן לְמַעֲשֶׂה בְּרֵאשִׁית

My best guess at the meaning of this prayer is:

_____

_____

זֵכֶר לִיצִיאַת מִצְרָיִם

My best guess at the meaning of this prayer is:

_____

_____

108

Ten Commandments Twice

The Ten Commandments are stated twice in the Torah. They are just about the same except for the שַׁבָּת commandment. To understand the קִדּוּשׁ, one must know the differences between the two sets of commandments.

Deuteronomy 5:12-13

שָׁמוֹר (observe) the שַׁבָּת to keep it holy....
Six days you can labor and do all your work
but the seventh day is a שַׁבָּת of the Eternal, your God....
Remember you were a slave in the Land of Egypt and the Eternal, your God, freed you from there....
Therefore, the Eternal, your God, commanded you to make שַׁבָּת.

Exodus 20:8-11

זָכוֹר (remember) the שַׁבָּת to keep it holy.
Six days you can labor and do all your work
but the seventh day is a שַׁבָּת of the Eternal, your God....
For in six days, the Eternal made heaven and earth and sea...and rested on the seventh day.
Therefore, the Eternal blessed שַׁבָּת and made it holy.

עֲצֹר!

Questions
1. How are the two commandments the same? How are they different?
2. Look at the full קִדּוּשׁ for שַׁבָּת on page 104. See what parts of the two versions of the Ten Commandments you can find.

Go back to page 104 and read the קִדּוּשׁ before you work on this page.

Use this page to do a variety of tasks. Have students read across the rows. Call on a student to read the text in a particular box (for example, "Yosi, please read the text in נ-שְׁתַּיִם"). Or play a game by asking students to assemble prayers or בְּרָכוֹת, pulling text from various boxes.

	ד	ג	ב	א
1 אַחַת	זֵכֶר לִיצִיאַת מִצְרָיִם	אֱלֹהֵינוּ מֶלֶךְ הָעוֹלָם	בָּרְכוּ אֶת יְיָ הַמְבֹרָךְ	יוֹצֵר אוֹר וּבוֹרֵא חֹשֶׁךְ
2 שְׁתַּיִם	וְהָאֵר עֵינֵינוּ בְּתוֹרָתֶךָ	בּוֹרֵא פְּרִי הַגָּפֶן	בָּרוּךְ אַתָּה יְיָ אֱלֹהֵינוּ מֶלֶךְ הָעוֹלָם	שֶׁהַכֹּל נִהְיֶה בִּדְבָרוֹ
3 שָׁלֹשׁ	מִי־כָמֹכָה בָּאֵלִים יְיָ	כִּי בָנוּ בָחַרְתָּ וְאוֹתָנוּ קִדַּשְׁתָּ מִכָּל הָעַמִּים	לְהַדְלִיק נֵר שֶׁל יוֹם טוֹב	וְאָהַבְתָּ אֵת יְיָ אֱלֹהֶיךָ
4 אַרְבַּע	עֹשֶׂה שָׁלוֹם וּבוֹרֵא אֶת הַכֹּל	בּוֹרֵא פְּרִי הָעֵץ	זִכָּרוֹן לְמַעֲשֵׂה בְרֵאשִׁית	הַמּוֹצִיא לֶחֶם מִן הָאָרֶץ
5 חָמֵשׁ	בְּכָל־לְבָבְךָ וּבְכָל־נַפְשְׁךָ וּבְכָל־מְאֹדֶךָ	אֲשֶׁר קִדְּשָׁנוּ בְּמִצְוֹתָיו וְצִוָּנוּ	שְׁמַע יִשְׂרָאֵל יְיָ אֱלֹהֵינוּ יְיָ אֶחָד	וְדַבֵּק לִבֵּנוּ בְּמִצְוֹתֶךָ

Shimon and Reuben See Mud

This story comes from the Midrash. Six hundred thousand Jews escaped from Egypt. Two of them were Shimon and Reuben. When the Reed Sea divided, 599,998 Jews were filled with wonder. They saw the water stop flowing. They saw dry land emerge. As they watched, huge flows of water froze into solid walls—it was a miracle.

Shimon and Reuben were looking at their feet. Shimon complained, "For years I had to work with mud. I had to go down into the mud and get my feet dirty. I took the mud and made it into bricks. This is some freedom—here I am still in the mud."

Reuben agreed. "We have to walk too far. If God wanted to do a miracle, God could have carried us back to Canaan. But instead we have to walk. Walking through mud is much harder, and my feet hurt."

Everyone else walked along with open mouths, totally amazed at how God had stopped nature and made a miracle. For Shimon and Reuben there were no miracles, there was just mud.

A Midrash

Questions

1. What made Shimon and Reuben different from the rest of Israel?
2. When are you like Shimon and Reuben?
3. When are you like the rest of Israel?
4. How can remembering this story help you to point your heart when you say the קָדוֹשׁ?

A Review

Some things to remember about the קִדּוּשׁ

- The קִדּוּשׁ is made up of two בְּרָכוֹת, which are said during שַׁבָּת or other Jewish holidays.

- The first בְּרָכָה is the בְּרָכָה over wine (or liquid other than water). The second בְּרָכָה talks about the holiness of this special day.

- The קִדּוּשׁ for שַׁבָּת is built around two ideas we are supposed to remember. One is that God brought us out of Egypt. The other is that God created the world. Both are good reasons to celebrate שַׁבָּת.

- The Ten Commandments are found in two different places in the Torah. In each place a different reason is given for celebrating שַׁבָּת. The קִדּוּשׁ brings both reasons together.

Language Learning

Some of the words we learned or reviewed in this lesson were:

קִדֵשׁ   מִצְרַיִם   יָצָא   פְּרִי הַגָּפֶן   עוֹלָם   מֶלֶךְ   אַתָּה   בָּרוּךְ

We learned and reviewed the following roots: קדשׁ and זכר.

Prayer Parts

We looked at four short parts of the קִדּוּשׁ:

We reviewed the בְּרָכָה over wine.

בָּרוּךְ אַתָּה יי אֱלֹהֵינוּ מֶלֶךְ הָעוֹלָם בּוֹרֵא פְּרִי הַגָּפֶן.

We reviewed the formula for בְּרָכוֹת over מִצְוֹת that begins the second בְּרָכָה.

בָּרוּךְ אַתָּה יי אֱלֹהֵינוּ מֶלֶךְ הָעוֹלָם אֲשֶׁר קִדְּשָׁנוּ בְּמִצְוֹתָיו...

We looked at the two phrases about memory.

זֵכֶר לִיצִיאַת מִצְרַיִם   זִכָּרוֹן לְמַעֲשֵׂה בְרֵאשִׁית

We quickly translated the end of the בְּרָכָה:

בָּרוּךְ אַתָּה יי מְקַדֵּשׁ הַשַּׁבָּת.

עֲצֹר!

112

מוֹדֶה אֲנִי

מוֹדֶה אֲנִי is a wake-up prayer. It is designed to be the first words that a Jew says upon waking. Later, it was also added to the beginning of the morning service.

מוֹדֶה אֲנִי

- thanks God for returning our soul,
- makes our connection to God our first thought of the day,
- reminds us that we can count on God,
- says that every day we get to start over.

Part of the traditional prayer we say at bedtime comes from the books of Psalms. We ask God to take care of our soul while we sleep. We say, "Into Your hands I place my soul." In the morning, we say **מוֹדֶה אֲנִי** to thank God for watching over our soul and for returning it to us.

In this unit you will learn
- about מוֹדֶה אֲנִי
- the root י ד ח
- one story about new beginnings.

Can you see the two letters חי in these words?

חַיֵינוּ   לְחַיִים   חַי

Sometimes Hebrew builds words out of two-letter roots.

חַיֵינוּ = our lives

לְחַיִים = to life

חַי = live

Recite these phrases and circle all the words that contain the root חי.

1. מוֹדֶה אֲנִי לְפָנֶיךָ מֶלֶךְ חַי וְקַיָּם

2. וְכָתְבֵנוּ בְּסֵפֶר הַחַיִים לְמַעַנְךָ אֱלֹהִים חַיִים.

3. מְכַלְכֵּל חַיִים בְּחֶסֶד, מְחַיֶּה מֵתִים בְּרַחֲמִים רַבִּים.

4. וְנֶאֱמָן אַתָּה לְהַחֲיוֹת מֵתִים. בָּרוּךְ אַתָּה יי מְחַיֶּה הַמֵּתִים.

5. וְנֶאֱמָן אַתָּה לְהַחֲיוֹת הַכֹּל. בָּרוּךְ אַתָּה יי מְחַיֶּה הַכֹּל.

6. צוּר חַיֵינוּ מָגֵן יִשְׁעֵנוּ אַתָּה הוּא לְדוֹר וָדוֹר.

7. בָּרוּךְ אַתָּה יי אֱלֹהֵינוּ מֶלֶךְ הָעוֹלָם שֶׁהֶחֱיָנוּ וְקִיְּמָנוּ וְהִגִּיעָנוּ לַזְּמַן הַזֶּה.

8. וּשְׁמוֹר צֵאתֵנוּ וּבוֹאֵנוּ לְחַיִים וּלְשָׁלוֹם מֵעַתָּה וְעַד עוֹלָם.

אֲנִי

מֶלֶךְ

Your teacher will help you with your translation.

thanks   you   before   and continuing

מוֹדֶה (מוֹדָה) אֲנִי לְפָנֶיךָ מֶלֶךְ חַי וְקַיָּם

that You   returned   me   in   my soul   in   kindness   great   faithfulness   Your

שֶׁהֶחֱזַרְתָּ בִּי נִשְׁמָתִי בְּחֶמְלָה רַבָּה אֱמוּנָתֶךָ.

My best guess at the meaning of this prayer is:

_____

_____

_____

To Talk About

Rabbi Ḥelbo said, "Every day God creates a new set of angels who sing a brand new song of praise to God. מוֹדֶה אֲנִי tells us that every day we wake up to a new adventure, a new set of possibilities, and a new chance to connect to God."

How can knowing that God creates new angels every morning help you to point your heart when you say מוֹדֶה אֲנִי?

עֲצֹר!

115

Go back to page 115 and read the מוֹדֶה אֲנִי before you work on this page.

Prayers with Something in Common

At the beginning of the service we say מוֹדֶה אֲנִי.
Near the end of the service, in the עֲמִידָה, we say a
very similar prayer, מוֹדִים אֲנַחְנוּ לָךְ.
מוֹדֶה אֲנִי is a prayer that each person says alone.
מוֹדִים אֲנַחְנוּ לָךְ is a prayer that talks about the
whole congregation.

See how many similar words you can find in each
line of מוֹדֶה אֲנִי and the first sentence of
מוֹדִים אֲנַחְנוּ לָךְ.

Hint: To review meaning, turn back to
page 115.

1. מוֹדֶה אֲנִי לְפָנֶיךָ
   מוֹדִים אֲנַחְנוּ לָךְ

What idea do the two סִדוּר sentences have
in common?

_____

_____

2. מֶלֶךְ חַי וְקַיָּם
   מֶלֶךְ הָעוֹלָם, שֶׁהֶחֱיָנוּ וְקִיְּמָנוּ

What idea do the two סִדוּר sentences have in
common?

_____

_____

3. שֶׁהֶחֱזַרְתָּ בִּי נִשְׁמָתִי בְּחֶמְלָה
   הַמַּחֲזִיר שְׁכִינָתוֹ

What idea do the two סִדוּר sentences have in
common?

_____

_____

4. רַבָּה אֱמוּנָתֶךָ
   אַהֲבָה רַבָּה אֲהַבְתָּנוּ

What idea do the two סִדוּר sentences have in
common?

_____

_____

The Shoes that Got Turned Around

Long ago, in a little village in the woods, there lived a girl who was angry with her family. This girl decided to run away from home, so she threw everything she owned into a napkin and tied the napkin to a stick. She put on her cloak, put the stick over her shoulder, and started walking. She walked all day, stopping only for a little lunch. Then, as it got to be dark, she stopped again and took out a little supper. Then she got ready to go to sleep. She took off her shoes and pointed them in the direction she needed to go in the morning. She covered herself with the cloak and went to sleep.

Somehow, while she slept, her shoes were turned around. Maybe a trickster came along and turned them. Maybe it was an angel. Maybe an animal nudged them. We will never know. In the morning the girl woke up, ate the last of the food, put on her cloak, her shoes, and continued walking in the direction her shoes pointed. She walked all day and came to a village in

the woods. It looked a lot like her village, but it was more colorful and more interesting. She walked down a street and saw a woman who looked a lot like her mother. The woman smiled at her and welcomed her the way she wished her mother would. She went into the woman's house and became part of this new family that was very much like her family, but at the same time different. She felt very much at home because this new home was everything she wanted her home to be. And so she lived happily ever after.

Questions

1. What had changed when the girl came back to her own home at the end of the story?
2. Did she come back to the same village or did she arrive in a different place?
3. How can remembering this story help you to point your heart when you say מוֹדֶה אֲנִי?
   (Hint: How is getting your soul back in the morning like having your shoes turned around?)

A Review

Some things to remember about מוֹדֶה אֲנִי

- מוֹדֶה אֲנִי is a prayer that was written to be said when a person wakes up. Later it was decided to also say it at the beginning of the morning service.

- מוֹדֶה אֲנִי speaks of our soul coming back every morning. It is a prayer that tries to get us to see every day as a new beginning.

Language Learning

Some of the words we learned or reviewed in this lesson were:

a lot	soul	and continuing	before		
רַבָּה	נְשָׁמָה	קַיָּם	לִפְנֵי	מֶלֶךְ	אֲנִי

And we learned the root חִ י .

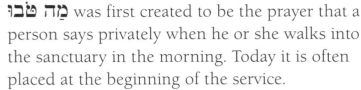

מַה טֹבוּ

מַה טֹבוּ was first created to be the prayer that a person says privately when he or she walks into the sanctuary in the morning. Today it is often placed at the beginning of the service.

מַה טֹבוּ is a collection of five biblical verses that are put together. The first of these verses is Numbers 24.5, which tells the story of Bilaam.

The second sentence in מַה טֹבוּ has ten words:

וַאֲנִי בְּרֹב חַסְדְּךָ אָבוֹא בֵיתֶךָ
אֶשְׁתַּחֲוֶה אֶל הֵיכַל קָדְשְׁךָ בְּיִרְאָתֶךָ

Often this verse is used to find out if there is a minyan. We say this sentence— a person with each word—rather than counting with numbers.

מַה טֹבוּ is a prayer that:

• helps us turn from our outside lives to a prayer space;

• reminds us that while a synagogue is a holy place, we need to find a holy space inside us for our prayers to make a difference;

• helps us to be like Bilaam, moving from anger and frustration into a time for blessing.

In this unit you will learn
• about מַה טֹבוּ
• the root שׁבן
• one story about Bilaam.

מַה טֹּבוּ

Wow, Jacob, your TENTS are good!	מַה טֹּבוּ אֹהָלֶיךָ יַעֲקֹב	1.
(So) are your DWELLINGS, Israel.	מִשְׁכְּנֹתֶיךָ יִשְׂרָאֵל.	2.
As for me—	וַאֲנִי	3.
I, THROUGH YOUR great KINDNESS,	בְּרֹב חַסְדְּךָ	4.
WILL COME to Your HOUSE.	אָבוֹא בֵיתֶךָ	5.
I WILL BOW to Your holy SANCTUARY	אֶשְׁתַּחֲוֶה אֶל הֵיכַל קָדְשְׁךָ	6.
in awe of You.	בְּיִרְאָתֶךָ.	7.
ADONAI	יי	8.
I love the protection of Your HOUSE.	אָהַבְתִּי מְעוֹן בֵּיתֶךָ	9.
and the TABERNACLE where Your honor dwells.	וּמְקוֹם מִשְׁכַּן כְּבוֹדֶךָ.	10.
AS FOR ME—I WILL BOW AND I WILL BEND	וַאֲנִי אֶשְׁתַּחֲוֶה וְאֶכְרָעָה,	11.
I WILL KNEEL (and bless)	אֶבְרְכָה	12.
before ADONAI, The One-Who-Makes me.	לִפְנֵי יי עֹשִׂי.	13.
As for me—	וַאֲנִי	14.
I (wish that) my prayer be before you, ADONAI,	תְפִלָּתִי לְךָ יי	15.
at an acceptable time.	עֵת רָצוֹן.	16.
God	אֱלֹהִים	17.
THROUGH YOUR great kindness	בְּרָב חַסְדֶּךָ	18.
ANSWER ME with the truth of Your deliverance.	עֲנֵנִי בֶּאֱמֶת יִשְׁעֶךָ.	19.

מַה טֹּבוּ tells the history of Jewish worship. It starts with the Tabernacle, the portable worship tent Jews used as a sanctuary in the wilderness. The prayer mentions the House, the Holy Temple, which King Solomon built in Jerusalem. These are connected to our own place of prayer (Kimmelman).

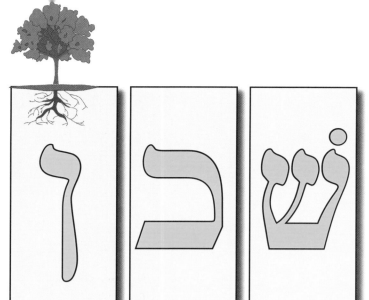

Can you see שָׁכַן in these words?

מִשְׁכָּן ְ שְׁכִינָה ְ מִשְׁכְּנֹתֶיךָ

Hebrew builds words out of three-letter roots.

Tabernacle = מִשְׁכָּן

the neighborly = שְׁכִינָה
part of God

your living places = מִשְׁכְּנֹתֶיךָ

Recite these phrases and circle all the words that contain the root שָׁכַן.

1. מַה טֹבוּ אֹהָלֶיךָ יַעֲקֹב, מִשְׁכְּנֹתֶיךָ יִשְׂרָאֵל.

2. יי אָהַבְתִּי מְעוֹן בֵּיתֶךָ וּמְקוֹם מִשְׁכַּן כְּבוֹדֶךָ.

3. בָּרוּךְ יי מִצִּיוֹן, שֹׁכֵן יְרוּשָׁלַיִם הַלְלוּיָהּ.

4. שׁוֹכֵן עַד מָרוֹם וְקָדוֹשׁ שְׁמוֹ.

5. בָּרוּךְ אַתָּה יי הַמַּחֲזִיר שְׁכִינָתוֹ לְצִיוֹן.

6. וְתִמְלֹךְ אַתָּה יי לְבַדֶּךָ עַל כָּל-מַעֲשֶׂיךָ בְּהַר צִיוֹן מִשְׁכַּן כְּבוֹדֶךָ.

Write in the missing letters for these words built from the root שָׁכַן.

9. מִשְׁכָּ__ __ 8. שְׁ__ __ינָתוֹ 7. __ __וֵן

12. __ __כוּנָה 11. שָׁ__ __ן 10. מִשְׁכְּ__ __תֶיךָ

121

טוב

אֹהֶל

שָׁכֵן

יִשְׂרָאֵל

Your teacher will help you with your translation.

מַה טֹּבוּ אֹהָלֶיךָ יַעֲקֹב, מִשְׁכְּנֹתֶיךָ יִשְׂרָאֵל.

My best guess at the meaning of this prayer is:

_____

_____

_____

(words)

how = מַה

Jacob = יַעֲקֹב

(word parts)

your = ךָ

To Talk About

There is a midrash that says that what changed Bilaam's mind was the way Israel set up its tents. Each and every tent was set up so that its door faced in a private direction. No one was able to look into another family's tent. Each family had its own private place. This midrash says that what changed Bilaam's mind was the respect that each Jew showed for the other.

What other things can a Jewish community do to make sure that everyone is treated with respect?

עֲצֹר!

122

Go back to page 120 and practice the מַה טֹבוּ before you work on this page.

Some Words Have Endings

Match the words on the right with those on the left that have ךָ endings.

מִשְׁכְּנֹתֶיךָ	אֹהָלִים
חַסְדְּךָ	יִרְאָה
בֵּיתֶךָ	כָּבוֹד
כְּבוֹדֶךָ	קֹדֶשׁ
אֹהָלֶיךָ	חֶסֶד
קָדְשְׁךָ	מִשְׁכָּנוֹת
יִרְאָתֶךָ	בַּיִת

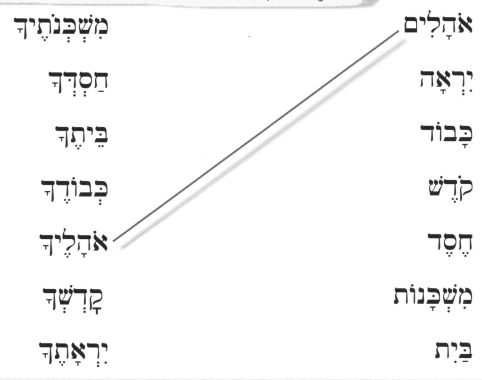

Back to Our Roots 1

Circle the words on each line that are built from the root word in the colored box.

הַמְּאוֹרוֹת זְרוּעַ וְהָאֵר תּוֹרָתוֹ אַהֲבָה	אוֹר	.1
הַבְּרִיּוֹת בִּרְכוֹת וּלְיִרְאָה נְבָרֵךְ יוֹצֵר	בּרך	.2
אָבִינוּ אֲהַבְתָּנוּ אֶת אֲבוֹתֵינוּ וְאָהַבְתָּ	אהב	.3
בְּמִצְוֹתֶךָ כַּנְפוֹת וְדָבֵק וְצִוָּנוּ עֵינֵינוּ	צוה command	.4
וְכָתְבֵנוּ לְחַיִּים מְחַיֶּה שֶׁהֶחֱיָנוּ מֵתִים	חי life	.5

123

Bilaam Says מַה טֹּבוּ

At the end of forty years in the wilderness, Israel was marching toward the land of Canaan. They wanted to follow a major road that led through the country of Moab. Balak, the king, didn't want 600,000 homeless people walking through his country, so he hired Bilaam, a wizard, to stop them with a curse.

Balak sent messengers to Bilaam and offered him a room full of gold to curse Israel. Bilaam asked God for permission and got a big "No." Balak then offered Bilaam two rooms full of gold. This time God told Bilaam, "You can go, but don't say anything that I don't tell you to say."

Bilaam got up in the morning and headed off to see Balak. Three times, God put an invisible angel with a sword in front of Bilaam's donkey and drove it off the road. Each time, Bilaam fell off the donkey. That didn't stop him. He picked himself up and beat the donkey. God made the donkey talk to Bilaam. "Listen, you have been riding me for years, and I have never acted like this before. Turn around and look."

It was then that he saw an angel with a sword of fire that God had placed in the road. The angel told him, "Don't say anything that God doesn't tell you to say."

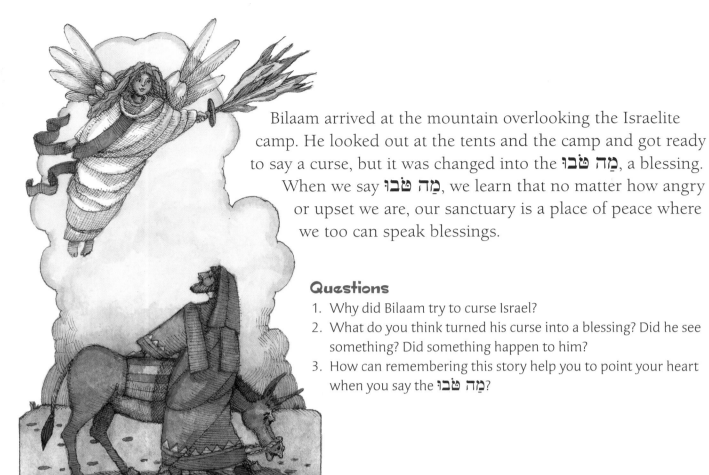

Bilaam arrived at the mountain overlooking the Israelite camp. He looked out at the tents and the camp and got ready to say a curse, but it was changed into the מַה טֹּבוּ, a blessing. When we say מַה טֹּבוּ, we learn that no matter how angry or upset we are, our sanctuary is a place of peace where we too can speak blessings.

Questions

1. Why did Bilaam try to curse Israel?
2. What do you think turned his curse into a blessing? Did he see something? Did something happen to him?
3. How can remembering this story help you to point your heart when you say the מַה טֹּבוּ?

Back to Our Roots 2

Circle the words on each line that are built from the root in the colored box.

create .1	בּרא	לִבְרֹא	רַבָּה	בְּרוּכִים	בְּרִיאָה	בְּרֵאשִׁית	
.2	קדשׁ	מְזוּזָה	קִדְּשָׁנוּ	לְהַדְלִיק	וְצִוָּנוּ	מְקַדֵּשׁ	
.3	מלך	מִצְוָה	לְבָבֵנוּ	הַמְּלָכִים	מַלְכֵּנוּ	לִבֵּנוּ	
.4	שׁמע	הִשְׁמִיעָנוּ	שֶׁמָּא	שְׁמוֹ	לִשְׁמֹעַ	הַשְּׂמֹאל	
.5	זכר	לְמַעֲשֶׂה	זִכָּרוֹן	לִיצִיאַת	בְּמִצְוֺתָיו	זָכְרֵנוּ	

125

1. מַה טֹּבוּ אֹהָלֶיךָ יַעֲקֹב מִשְׁכְּנֹתֶיךָ יִשְׂרָאֵל וַאֲנִי בְּרֹב חַסְדְּךָ

2. אוֹר חָדָשׁ עַל צִיּוֹן תָּאִיר וְנִזְכֶּה כֻלָּנוּ מְהֵרָה לְאוֹרוֹ

3. וְהָאֵר עֵינֵינוּ בְּתוֹרָתֶךָ וְדַבֵּק לִבֵּנוּ בְּמִצְוֹתֶיךָ וְיַחֵד לְבָבֵנוּ לְאַהֲבָה

4. אַהֲבָה רַבָּה אֲהַבְתָּנוּ יי אֱלֹהֵינוּ חֶמְלָה גְדוֹלָה וִיתֵרָה חָמַלְתָּ עָלֵינוּ

5. וְשִׁנַּנְתָּם לְבָנֶיךָ וְדִבַּרְתָּ בָּם בְּשִׁבְתְּךָ בְּבֵיתֶךָ וּבְלֶכְתְּךָ בַדֶּרֶךְ

6. צוּר יִשְׂרָאֵל קוּמָה בְּעֶזְרַת יִשְׂרָאֵל וּפְדֵה כִנְאֻמֶךָ יְהוּדָה וְיִשְׂרָאֵל

7. וְשַׁבַּת קָדְשׁוֹ בְּאַהֲבָה וּבְרָצוֹן הִנְחִילָנוּ זִכָּרוֹן לְמַעֲשֵׂה בְרֵאשִׁית

A Review

Some things to remember about the מַה טֹּבוּ

- מַה טֹּבוּ is a prayer with a story. It is the story of how God turned Bilaam's curse into a blessing. We use מַה טֹּבוּ to begin our services to make sure that our words are turned into blessings.

- We use the second sentence in מַה טֹּבוּ to assemble a minyan. The מַה טֹּבוּ helps us turn the room in which we have gathered into a place of worship.

Language Learning

Some of the words we learned or reviewed in this lesson were:

what

יִשְׂרָאֵל   שָׁכֵן   אֹהֶל   טוֹב   מַה

עֲצֹר!

and we learned the root .

126

A Review

Match the prayer with the image of the prayer.

אַהֲבָה רַבָּה

מוֹדֶה אֲנִי

מַה טֹבוּ

בָּרְכוּ

יוֹצֵר אוֹר

שְׁמַע

קָדוֹשׁ

וְאָהַבְתָּ

מִי־כָמֹכָה

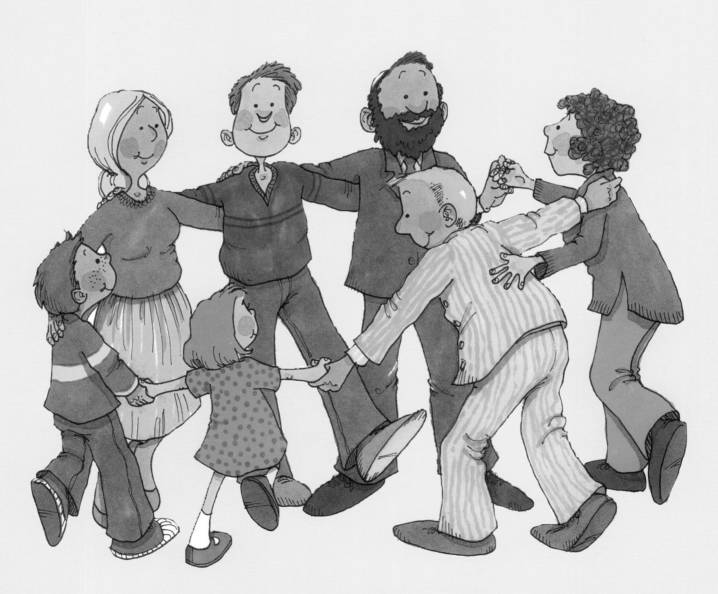